SPIRIT ANIMALS AND THE WHEEL OF LIFE

Books by Hal Zina Bennett

Follow Your Bliss, with Susan J. Sparrow.

Holotropic Mind: the Three Levels of Human Consciousness and How They Shape Our Lives, with Stanislav Grof

Lens of Perception: The Shamanic Vision in Everyday Life

Mind Jogger: A Problem Solving Companion

Spirit Circle: A Story of Adventure and Shamanic Revelation

Well Body Book, with Mike Samuels, M.D.

Well Body, Well Earth: The Sierra Club Environmental Health Sourcebook with Mike Samuels, M.D.

Write from the Heart: Unleashing the Power of Creativity

Zuni Fetishes: Using Native American Objects for Meditation, Reflection, and Insight

SPIRIT ANIMALS AND THE WHEEL OF LIFE

HAL ZINA BENNETT

HAMPTON ROADS
PUBLISHING COMPANY, INC.

Cover art and design by BrickerGraphics
Illustrations by Angela Wenneke

Hampton Roads Publishing Company, Inc.
Charlottesville, VA 22906
www.hrpub.com

If you are unable to order this book from your local
bookseller, you may order directly from the publisher.
Call 434-296-2772.

Library of Congress Catalog Card Number: 00-110847

ISBN 978-1-57174-216-2
10 9 8 7 6 5 4 3
Printed on acid-free paper in the United States

Help me to speak my own truth quietly, to listen with an open mind when others speak, and to remember the peace that comes with silence.

Cherokee Prayer of Good Counsel

Contents

Introduction:

Opening Inward

More than four decades have passed since my then-young life took an unexpected turn, one that would lead me far from my Middle-American roots. During a serious illness (see chapter 3), I stood for two days at a junction between life and death, and during that time I glimpsed a reality that nobody in my everyday world could explain. Indeed, I did not even know what questions to ask! Following my recovery, I met teachers who challenged every value and convention I had ever been taught. I listened, even sought these teachers out, because they offered insights into, or at least some peace of mind about, what I'd experienced during my illness.

The first teacher was not a human but an animal. He was a beautiful white buck who appeared to me during a hunting trip in northern Michigan. It was no dream or vision, but a real deer. In spite of the fact that it was the middle of deer season, when the animals are particularly fearful, he stopped within fifty feet of me. He stared me down as I sat there with my rifle in my lap, apparently knowing that I would not shoot him.

The truth is that I wasn't even tempted to raise my rifle, because what I saw in this animal's eyes and in its very presence was something far more important than the meat he would provide for our table or a trophy to show off to my friends. What I saw in his gaze connected with something I had experienced as I hovered between life and death nearly a year before. The impression was one of being joined with a force much greater than myself. At least twenty years later, I would be reminded of this moment when I met the great spiritual teacher Muktananda. This man had spent a lifetime seeking the connection with a higher truth that his presence emanated. The deer had come into life with this connection.

Soon after the encounter with the white deer, I learned that the indigenous peoples of the area considered the white buck a sacred animal that usually appeared only during vision quests. This did not mean a great deal to me at the time since I had no vocabulary to make sense of it. I thought it a strange superstition, and though my encounter with this animal was during an extreme personal crisis, I took it only as a meaningless coincidence.

Along with this experience, I also received an ancient artifact—a beautifully crafted tomahawk head that my fingers had closed around as I sat down under a tree just before the white deer visited me. This tomahawk held the energy of the person who had carved it, and of a way of life long past. As I held it in my hand, I slipped into a daydream in which I saw a man shaping this tool by chipping away with a harder rock. The tomahawk head immortalized the craftsman's efforts, and even to this day, I feel a special privilege in possessing his handiwork.

These two events—the encounter with the white deer and finding the artifact—had a dramatic affect on me. When I tried to tell friends about the deer, however, I was chastised for "freezing up," for being a bad hunter, before I could manage to tell them what I'd experienced in that encounter. And when I tried to talk about the tomahawk head, the same friends told me how I could sell it to a collector and get a lot of money. As they spoke, I began doubting what I'd experienced and felt there must be something wrong with me for making so much of it.

For many years after that, I kept my mouth shut about such experiences, largely to protect myself from ridicule. I knew there was much more to these events than meat, trophies or money, but I had nothing to base this knowledge on. Meanwhile, I wondered if I was just a fool, completely out of step with my peers.

Six or eight years after my encounter with the white deer, I met a shaman who taught me how to journey to inner space and begin probing the mysteries of what he called "the unseen reality." At the time, I had no idea what a shaman was or what his function might be as a spiritual teacher. What I did understand was that for the first time in my life I was on the right path. The experiences I had during non-ordinary states of consciousness allowed me to better understand what I had encountered years before when I was very ill. I also recognized that my encounter with the white deer and the gift of the tomahawk head had been subtle teachings that I would understand better in the years ahead.

Even with the help I'd received, I was highly skeptical of what I was discovering in this other realm. Spiritual revelation aside, how did one incorporate such insights into everyday life? For example: psychology teaches that love is a human emotion, yet there are certain shamanic experiences which I feel demonstrate beyond a shadow of a doubt that love is a universal force, independent of human perception. It is the key catalyst of Creation itself. But how do we make use of that in our daily lives, given our human limitations and general pettiness?

Forty some years have passed since those first encounters with the unseen reality, and on most days I can honestly say that any doubts I once had about that reality have faded away. I have been blessed with many teachers since those early years, some from the world of everyday life, but as often as not, from the world of the unseen. Some teachers have been human, but it has increasingly been the lessons of the animals which have meant the most to me.

Readers who know my other books may be familiar with my previous efforts to deal with some of these subjects covered in *Spirit Guides, The Lens of Perception, Zuni Fetishes,* and *Spirit Circle.* But *Spirit Animals and the Wheel of Life* is my first attempt to describe the spiritual practice that has evolved as a result of my journey. To be honest, this has not been an easy book to write. Being a private person, I feel protective of my daily spiritual practice. In many ways it is nobody's business but my own. However, over the past three years my teachers have pushed me toward writing about it. There is, I feel, an increasing urgency to learn about, and to embrace a spiritual viewpoint that will help combat the desecration of our home planet. It is more important than ever to hold the position that the assaults on Mother Earth, which get more vicious each day, are a hideous sacrilege in addition to being environmentally dangerous.

I offer *Spirit Animals and the Wheel of Life* as a way to begin reclaiming your own ecospiritual connection with our planet—not just as a philosophy but as a practical spirituality and a way of mapping your own path back to the center. The practices I describe are drawn from many traditions. The wheel of life has many names and many different manifestations but the basic configuration (the wheel or circle) is found throughout the world. It can take the form of a sacred circle, a labyrinth, or a medicine wheel. Whatever the form, it always helps us to reflect on the continuum of spirit, manifesting again and again, apparently without beginning or end. It teaches us how to work with the limits of human knowing and how to find peace with our apparent human differences.

The rest of the map that I present here is drawn from observing the natural world and studying those principles of human life which certain animals teach us. I see these animals as spirit teachers, helping us to understand the influences of the wheel's seven positions (described later). Whether it be the new beginnings of a rising sun, or closure with the setting sun at the end of the day, or the familial love of a community of wolves in the wild, each of these is a primal influence that touches all of our lives. And they all take permanent positions on the wheel of life.

To know these principles of the natural order is to know ourselves at the most primal levels. With these principles as our coordinates, we can find our way back to the center on whatever path we are given.

In a way, this book teaches a kind of "spiritual orienteering." Like the magnetized needle of the compass that orients us to the north, the symbols, insights, and guides that I describe here will help you understand where you are and how to get where you need to be. Nothing I offer is so sacred, however, that you cannot find another icon to replace it, one that perhaps speaks more crisply and clearly to you. I intend only to offer a model in a world where such models are few and far between.

The model I offer is one that many people will associate with the shamanic tradition. While that may be true, I caution against labeling it as such. Labels too easily obscure understanding. Anthropologists in recent years have scientifically established what intuition has been telling us forever. They tell us that what we call shamanism is the oldest of religious practices, originating tens of thousands of years before any of the religions of today were formalized. Primitive drawings on cliffs, in caves, or on the ground itself attest to the fact that we humans have been exploring and paying homage to the unseen forces of the cosmos for as long as we have been able to reflect on our own lives.

Shamanism, as we understand it today, is simply another way of seeing, another way of looking at the world. As a process for observing and making sense of our lives, it is different from science, technology, philosophy, and even modern theology. It is different from psychology, sociology, anthropology, or any other "-ology," though it may observe the same things. If there is any definition that I feel comes even close to telling us anything useful, it would be that shamanism is a system of knowing that honors our own life experience, without mistaking it for the truth. And it is a way to embrace those invisible teachers who help us find grace in our dance between the seen and unseen worlds.

Animals have much to teach us. As does the tradition of the wheel of life. As do the Earth-based spiritual practices that reconnect us with the higher truths of our existence. Keys for our own personal and spiritual development can be found here. But even more than that, the practices described in these pages can guide our collective evolution by teaching us to listen for and honor a greater voice than the narrow focus of the human ego.

An Ecospiritual Journey into Space

> *There's so much for us to learn about spirituality, about loving the Earth, about choosing ecstasy over materialism, about ourselves, about oneness. The indigenous people have a great deal to teach us.*
>
> —John Perkins (Ausubel, 1997)

July of 1969 marked a turning point in human history. That year Neil Armstrong became the first human to set foot on the Moon. Visiting the Moon was clearly a stunning technological achievement. But something even more momentous happened during that and subsequent trips outside the Earth's atmosphere. For the first time we viewed our home planet from outer space and, as astronaut Rusty Schweickart would put it, it "made a difference in that relationship between you and that planet and you and all those other forms of life on that planet . . . (O'Leary 1989)" Our journeys to the stars turned us back to inner space and forced us to look more carefully at how we treat our planet and fellow inhabitants.

This may seem like an odd way to begin a book titled *Spirit Animals and The Wheel of Life*. But in fact, given our place in history it just might be a perfect start. It is no coincidence that soon after our penetration of space, we saw an upsurge of interest in ancient cultures, particularly the nature-based cultures that preceded modern technology by tens of thousands of years. Their teachings beckoned to us because nothing else promised to show us the way into the mysteries unsealed by our trip to the stars. Our outer journeys reconnected us with that first creature on Earth who gazed up at the heavens and was filled with wonder.

Books like those of Carlos Castaneda, which explore the world of modern day sorcery, became enormously popular, as did the books about medicine people such as Black Elk and John Lame Deer. Around the same time we saw an upsurge of interest in contemporary shamanism through the writings of Joan Halifax, Michael Harner, Sun Bear, Lynn Andrews, and others.

The view of the whole planet Earth from space symbolizes a birth of consciousness. As the astronauts gazed down on our seemingly colored marble in the black sea, they were transformed. The spectacular photographs they brought back … remind us poignantly that we have one very beautiful fragile planet to love and preserve. Our experience is unity.

—Brian O'Leary

So what is the link between these events—on the one hand this paradigm-shattering technological achievement, and on the other our turning back to the teachings of indigenous peoples? I'm convinced that the return to these earliest spiritual teachings has been instinctive, something reawakened in us by our view of our planet from outer space. Never before had we received visual proof of our interdependence with our planet. I say "interdependence" because never before has it been so clear that the way we treat Her will determine whether or not She continues to support us. Never before have we seen the oneness of all earthly life in quite the way we now do. We have instinctively turned to the ancient teachings because it is here that we might discover the mystical link between our beautiful blue planet, the Universe in which it rests, and ourselves.

The events which occurred that day we went to the Moon were not a surprise for everyone. Five hundred years before, Hopi elders had predicted that the white man would one day travel to the stars, and when he did the world would change dramatically—not necessarily for the better. When it happened there would be those who would recognize that something more than setting a technological benchmark had occurred. Some would see truths that reflected on human behavior, and on what our choices were doing to the planet. Astronaut Edgar Mitchell perhaps said it best when he reflected: "The crew of spacecraft Earth is in virtual mutiny to the order of the Universe." Is it possible to turn the mutineers around?

The Hopi prophets, as well as elders such as Black Elk from other indigenous cultures, predicted that soon after the white man penetrated space, Mother Earth would send warnings. The order of the Universe had been disrupted, and there would be those who would feel this acutely. Some people would seek help from the teachings of indigenous peoples, and there would be those from every ethnic background and race who would recognize the wisdom of the Hopi elders and would seek out their teachings and be bound to disseminating them.

New scientific findings are beginning to support beliefs of cultures thousands of years old, showing that our individual psyches are, in the last analysis, a manifestation of cosmic consciousness and intelligence that flows through all of existence. We never completely lose contact with this cosmic consciousness because we are never fully separated from it.

—Stanislav Grof

The pollution of air, water, and farmland, global warming—to say nothing of the nuclear threat—all put us on the alert that maybe the Hopi elders were right. It is impossible to ignore the increased numbers of floods, earthquakes, volcanic eruptions, famines, and devastating storms striking major populations worldwide. Surely it is time to change our vision, from domination to reverence, and from exploitation to recognition of the mystery of life itself.

There is a large portion of the human population now seeking new ways of relating to our planet and each other, and we are finding these methods in the ancient past. As with technology, new solutions will have to come from within, but this time from our hearts rather than just our heads—and from a universal rather than selfish perspective. Health and balance for the twenty-first century must be ecospiritual—integrating body, mind, and spirit, along with Earth.

In the heat of unprecedented technological breakthroughs it is easy to think that we are invincible, like gods who would rule the world. But none of us need be reminded that the future of our planet is being held hostage by our own cleverness, with nuclear physics, chemistry, agribusiness, mineral exploration, and bioengineering threatening our biosphere in ways we could never have imagined even twenty years ago.

At a Bioneers[1] Conference in 1995, author-lecturer Paul Hawken asked the audience to remember the final scenes in the movie *Close Encounters of the Third Kind* when the Earth scientists first made contact with the extraterrestrials: While the scientists played tones to communicate with several small space craft hovering around the area, excitement mounted. Then, the mother ship rose from out of

---

[1] The Bioneers are an ecology organization who are using nature to heal nature, working with individuals, organizations, communities, and governments to implement lasting change for a sustainable future.

nowhere, unbelievably massive, a titanic structure in the sky that was a world unto itself.

In recalling this scene, Paul Hawken likened the mother ship to the omnipotence of nature and the biological world. It hovers there, inconceivably large, and we become aware that it is not an insensate chunk of stuff that we can selfishly exploit or attempt to control—at least not without great consequence. Lacking a spiritual connection with it, we are doomed.

This sacred journey— understanding ourselves as a collective species in balance with the larger circle of vibrant life—allows us to reinvent ourselves in harmony with the majestic web of life.

—*Kenny Ausubel*

We need a new vision. We need to learn ways to live more in tune with nature's rhythms rather than attempting to impose our own. I like John Perkins' appeal, that we must "create a vision of a renewed society in tune with the natural world, imbued with spirit and devoted to the reenchantment of the Earth (Ausubel 1997)."

Our response to this planetary challenge thus far has been to turn to technology, and to the very mindsets that brought us to this point. We look at how we are abusing nature and seek technological ways to change what we've been doing. We invent less toxic pesticides, formulate less polluting fuels, design more efficient power plants, and begin recycling waste in our homes. While these things are important, we must ultimately see that our long term solutions are not primarily technological but ecospiritual, and based on awe, reverence, and conservation, rather than domination, exploitation, and control.

Luckily, we don't need to start from scratch in our quest for ecospiritual values to guide us. Systems of ecospirituality have been around far longer than the technological solutions we have employed so far—in fact, about 25,000 years longer. Nature-based societies began with the premise that Creation itself was an impenetrable mystery, and they were held in awe of it. Throughout the world, archaeologists have discovered petroglyphs and other art that provide us with clues about how ancient people experienced their lives, and what they did to honor the mystery. Drawings etched into rock walls with a crystal show that the shamans consulted the spirits of the animals, and apparently received vital guidance from them.

Those who recognize and honor our true kinship [with animals] begin to make very different kinds of choices, opting not to do things that would hurt the Earth or the creatures upon it, and instead choosing to live in harmony with all. This harmony extends to everything we do; from how we relate to each other to how we relate to great ecosystems such as the deserts or wetlands near our homes, to the distant Amazon rain forests, or the great oceans that lie between our continents.

—*The author*

About a year before I began writing this book, a feature article about shamanistic petroglyphs found in the Mojave Desert and dating back to at least 10,000 years before Christ appeared on the front pages of the *New York Times* (see: Graham 1998). At a meeting of the Society for California Archaeology, Larry Loendorf, a scholar of rock art from the New Mexico State University, confirmed that the recent Mojave Desert findings were consistent with spiritual practices at least 25,000 years old. As the earliest form of religion, these shamanistic practices drew inspiration from observing animals in nature.

Evidence of these early shamanistic religions has been found throughout the world, and each finding provides us with direction for integrating the mysteries of life on our planet with the practical challenges of everyday life. In the next chapter, I discuss the artwork found at the Lascaux caves in the south of France, a magnificent treasure trove of shamanistic art that dates back to Cro-Magnon times. Without going into too much detail here, suffice it to say that in these petroglyphs, we begin to find clues about how we might—12,000 years later—find the path to living with greater attunement to nature through looking to the animals as our teachers.

Whether we look to the Mojave Desert petroglyphs or to the paleolithic caves of Western Europe, it is clear that early peoples turned to animals as their teachers. Animals tutored them in everything from gathering in numbers against their adversaries to hunting. But even more than this, they found in the animals a conduit to Creation, to a power greater than themselves, greater than everything they beheld with their physical senses. This connection with higher truths gave their lives direction and purpose.

Each one of us still retains this awe that our ancient ancestors felt thousands of years ago. Most of the time, it hides deep within our psyches, ignored like a vestigial tail, making itself known to us through a vague, undefined longing that rises up in our dreams. It gets awakened when we visit the seashore or walk in the woods, or when we hold a newborn human or other animal baby. We touch it in deep meditation and prayer, and in quiet moments, sometimes at two A.M., when the whole world seems to be sleeping. We may try to dull the pain of our disconnection with drugs, alcohol, sex, sensationalism, or by blotting it out with high adrenaline activities and entertainments. Unrecognized, our lack of connectedness can drive us to indifference and rage; recognized, it can teach us how to reenchant our lives.

Many indigenous cultures offer artifacts, rituals, and ways of thinking about and experiencing our lives which have their spiritual roots in nature and can serve as beacons, giving direction at a time when humanity is on the brink of extinction. There is a growing consciousness of the Earth's needs—that She is crying out for our attention, and it is time to give it to Her. In this respect, turning to the ancient teachings is not about romanticizing or emulating others' ways of life, but is about finding our way back to a nurturing relationship with the universal order.

Joseph Campbell believed that our "voyages into outer space turn us back to inner space," and that through these voyages we discover that "we live in the stars and we are finally moved by awe to our greatest adventures." For many, this inner-space adventure takes us to a world where each individual soul at last feels its kinship with the higher power that nurtures us, and that created us. We recognize that we share this spiritual source with all of Creation—all plants, all animals, all beings, and the unfathomable plan manifest in the physical universe.

As I write these words I'm remembering a visit a few years ago from my friend Americo Yabar, who lives in Peru. We were sitting on my back porch talking, and he was watching my two small dogs romping around in the yard. Americo was not accustomed to pets like these. He beamed with delight as Cicely, the smaller dog, raced up to him, stood on her hind legs and licked his hand, begging him to pick her up.

Charmed by this behavior, Americo took the dog into his arms, hugging her to his chest. As he did so, he seemed to soften, to be transformed in a subtle way. Perhaps by embracing this tiny creature, my friend recalled his bonds with the wilderness of his home, thousands of miles to the south. I knew from previous conversations we'd had that when he visited my world of cement and manmade structures his heart ached for the bond he shared with the natural world of his beloved homeland.

Americo is a *paq'o* (spiritual teacher or shaman-priest) in the ancient *Q'ero* tradition, an indigenous people who make their home in the mountains high above Cuzco, Peru. It is said that they are descendants of the Inca holy men who escaped to the mountains when Pizarro routed their capital in 1533 in his search for gold.

Even very young children know that their world is populated by spirits—the mountain has a spirit, the river has a spirit, the tree has a spirit, the stone has a spirit.

—*Americo Yabar*

As Americo held the dog in his arms, he began telling stories about the long, steep trails into the mountains where, for thousands of years, the Q'ero have maintained a spiritual tradition that draws its deepest lessons from the Earth. For them, our planet is the *Pachamama*, that is, "Cosmic Mother."

My friend spoke of two realities that the Q'ero people recognize: the *panya* (pah-nyah) and the *yoqe* (yo-kay). Panya is all that we associate with the everyday reality of the senses, which is all around us—the surface features and interactions of the physical world. Yoqe is all that we associate with the unseen reality, with the world we cannot perceive with our senses; it is the mystery that connects us with the subtle energies that are present in all beings. In the ancient tradition from which the Q'ero draw, the spiritual teachings grow out of our dance between yoqe and panya, that is, between the mystery of the subtle, invisible energies that animate all life and our manifestation as physical beings living on the Earth.

High in the Andes a Q'ero child learns at an early age to speak with the plants, with the stones, with the animals, with the trees and mountains. She basks in the mystery, in the yoqe. And it is out of this close association with non-ordinary reality that girl finds the primordial roots of spiritual guidance.

As they grow into adulthood, the Q'ero continue to receive their primary teachings from their deeply intimate relationship with the Pachamama. The shaman-priest may help to guide people back to Pachamama, to encourage them to find answers there, not from the mouths of the teacher. They do not personify the higher powers of the cosmos as entities separate from them and superior to them, with whom they must communicate through a teacher, rather, they speak of an energy that flows throughout the whole Universe, animating all and accessible to all.

Americo and I have had many conversations before and after that afternoon on my back porch. But there was something special about that day for me. In those few hours of our visit, occasionally interrupted by the romping dogs, questions I had been pondering for years moved closer to resolution. The core question, which first troubled me when I was still in my teens, had to do with the tug I felt from the Earth, from the way nature speaks to us, not with words but with a subtler language that unveils a reality beyond what our senses can detect.

Talking with Americo, I was convinced that regardless of our family traditions, ethnic heritages or attachments to the modern world, we can learn to reconnect with the Pachamama. As much as these practices may be associated with cultures and religions outside our direct experience, they are not dictated by priests, shamans, philosophers, theologians, nations, or "-isms" of any kind. Moreover, times demand that we reach beyond our modern paradigms which have contributed so much to the crises we face today.

The guidance available to us through some of the most ancient Earth-centered practices owes its existence, not to a particular culture or group of elders, but to the singular force we all share, the source that animates all life—the Pachamama. Not one of us is separate from this source, though we may not understand how to span the distance we have created between us. The truths we seek ultimately come not from teachers or books or dogmas or rituals but from the awareness of our relationship with that infinite demiurge at the center of the greatest mystery of all.

What we are seeking has less to do with belief systems and religions than with the longing to reconnect with the mystery, with what we sometimes feel when we gaze into the night sky and contemplate infinite space beyond the stars, and wonder. . . .

Although they are quickly disappearing, threatened by the juggernaut of expanding populations, there are still hundreds, perhaps thousands, of communities of people following Earth-based spiritual traditions. They are holders of truths that must be reintegrated into all our lives if our planet, and all that the Pachamama supports, are to survive. It is necessary that we learn to hear the voices of these elders not only because they can take us to the past but because they can take us to the future.

2

Recognizing Animal Wisdom

> *The idea that we know ourselves through ani-*
> *mals appears again and again in the theories of*
> *the origins of consciousness. Some people say the*
> *animals once had all the knowledge and trans-*
> *mitted it to us. . . . Others say that human self-*
> *awareness begins in the caves, when our*
> *grandfathers and grandmothers marked the*
> *walls with animal images, making the first*
> *move from only-literal to also-imaginal.*
> —James Hillman (1997)

Throughout history animals have been seen as our teachers, even as deities. They are in Greek and Roman legends, in our zodiac, in our dreams, in Nordic and Celtic legends, in the arcane symbolism of Egypt, and even in Christian spiritual texts. In the latter, Job proclaims, "But ask now the beasts, and they shall teach thee; and the fowls of the air, and they shall teach thee . . . "(Job 12:7) Similarly, St. Francis of Assisi based his life's mission on the premise that it was through the kinship between humankind and the natural world that he was able to perform miracles.

For those of us immersed in a world of technology, grasping the concept of animals as teachers is not easy. We need to reach back almost to the beginning of history, letting ourselves be inspired by artifacts left behind by our distant relations who lived much closer to the natural world than we do. But where do we begin? Let me take you on a little journey:

The year is 1940 in the Dordogne region in the south of France. Four teenage boys decided to explore a cave in Lascaux that an old woman had told them about. The boys carried with them a kerosene lamp and ropes to lower themselves into the deep cavern that they found at the edge of a woods, just as the old woman had said. As they descended into the Earth, they came into a large cavern, and suddenly the fiery glow from their lamp revealed a vast panorama of graceful and lively paintings and engravings of animals. Wondrous murals of horses, deer, cattle, and bison adorned the ceilings, walls, and tunnels. There were species of animals no longer seen in this region, mysterious creatures from a very different time. Visions of a world they could not even imagine came to life, illuminated by the boys' lantern.

Little did they realize that they were looking at art dating back thousands of years to the Paleolithic period, and that their discovery would cause us to revise our understanding of the evolution of human consciousness. Until this remarkable discovery, scholars had believed our Cro-Magnon ancestors to be little more than brutish creatures whose main concern was survival.

Surely, the scholars had argued, these beings would not have been capable of anything we'd recognize as human feelings, and certainly they would not have been artists. Yet, the paintings in the cave at Lascaux are graphic evidence that our distant ancestors were quite capable of the finest renderings, proving that their mental and spiritual capacities were not unlike our own. In addition, they had left us a record of the close kinship they had with the natural world, which at least eight millennia later would reach out to teach us how to learn from the animals.

In the graceful, lively lines of running horses and flowing herds of deer, the observer is reminded of the forces of nature. I submit that the imagery of the animals expresses the artists' awareness of a power greater than themselves. Through these paintings, they probed the mystery of the spirit that gave these animals life, a source that the artists probably recognized they themselves had in common with all beasts.

Every creature is full of God and is a book about God.

—*Meister Eckhart*

The artists who decorated this cave so lovingly obviously found the creatures of nature to be worthy subjects for their art, but more than this, they quite possibly saw the imagery they created as religious icons, worthy of serious contemplation by generations of Cro-Magnon who visited this place for several hundred years. The Lascaux cave, like a paleolithic Sistine Chapel, celebrates the mysteries of life and also provides imagery that guides us back to the animals as our teachers.

Enter the Shaman Priest

These paintings illustrate the hunt, but they also tell us of a special relationship between the animals and the humans, something that has to do with the teachings of the natural world. A mysterious human figure stands beside a recently speared bison. Prominently displayed nearby is a bird perched on a stick. What are they doing here? Mircea Eliade, a leading authority on shamanism, who held the prestigious position of chairman of the Department of History of Religions at the University of Chicago, has noted that the archetypal symbol—the "soul-bird"—represents the shaman's magico-religious ability to extend his or her consciousness beyond the physical boundaries of everyday life, providing him with the power to travel into other realities. Eliade bases this observation on having compared the images at Lascaux with imagery from other shamanic traditions, some of which are still in existence today.

We now turn our attention to paintings and drawings from these traditions depicting figures which are part animal and part human—figures which at times seem to be danc-ing, probably performing rituals now long forgotten. The meaning of these figures is still open to speculation. But artifacts and stories of other shamanic cultures would indi-cate that they tell of the shaman's ability to transform himself into other species. Even today, shaman-priests merge with animals to gain the spiritual insight and under-standing that they believe the creatures possess.

The first time I witnessed this was with my friend Americo Yabar, whom I mentioned earlier. In the mountain villages above Cuzco where he was raised, he became known for having a special affinity for the puma, or mountain lions, which are numerous in the area. One day, a friend of Americo's came to him and asked him if he would bring a gun to shoot a puma that had been bothering his wife. Since Americo considers himself a brother of the puma, he was horrified at the thought and told the man that he would not kill the puma for any reason. However, he agreed to come and speak with the puma and find out what the problem was.

As the story goes, the puma only showed up when the man's wife was home alone. Then it would come and sit outside her door, perhaps a hundred feet away. When she came out to work in her garden, the puma followed her every move. This frightened the woman, of course, for she knew that puma could be dangerous if they felt threatened.

As Americo told me this story, he chuckled. "I think," he said, speaking in Spanish, "that the puma was in love with the man's wife." He found this quite amusing, but also said that he believed it could be true, that there were many stories of puma developing attachments to certain people.

Americo told his friends that he would camp out nearby, and the man would leave his house, setting off as if going to the next village, several hours away. When the puma came to visit, Americo planned to have a little talk with him.

As he continued to tell me his story, Americo's voice changed, becoming hushed and low. He described the puma's arrival, and as he did so Americo himself began moving and taking on the behavior of a cautious puma. He still was in the body of a man, of course, but every inch of him radiated *puma-ness*. I was actually frightened by the change in his manner.

When the puma saw Americo, he turned away from the woman and moved slowly toward the shaman, who simply waited patiently and unafraid. Finally, with only a few yards separating them, the puma halted. Staring the puma in the eye in what Americo described as a "loving but respectful" way, man told puma that he must stop visiting this woman. He was not wanted here, and besides, he should be looking for a partner of his own species.

The story ended here, but I had to ask, "Did the puma understand? Did he stay away after that?"

Americo laughed. "He did not come back!"

I told Americo that, during his story when he began taking on the movements and postures of a puma, I actually became a little frightened. He looked at me with a puzzled expression. He did not know what I was talking about. I said, "When you told about the puma coming, you began to move like a puma and look like one."

He shrugged. He didn't seem to understand why I was making so much of this. No, he said, it was not something he did for his audience—not a performance. When I pressed him to explain, he looked at me as if I was stupid. He finally said that if you are going to know an animal and learn from it, you naturally have to feel who he is with your muscles and bones. He could not imagine that I didn't know this, though I had to confess that I didn't.

One should pay attention to even the smallest crawling creatures, for these too may have a valuable lesson to teach us, and even the smallest ant may wish to communicate with a man.

—*Black Elk*

Through this way of experiencing the animal, we learn what it has to teach us. We touch its wisdom not by means of words or symbols and the intellect, but by what happens to us at a kinetic level, in the cells of our muscles and bones, in our movements and feelings. Might it be that this phenomenon is what Cro-Magnon artists were depicting in these part human, part animal figures? Remember, the images they have painted are not directly from life but from what was imprinted in their minds. No herds of animals posed in the cave for them, magically frozen in motion. They painted what they saw in their minds' eyes, what they had recorded in their muscles and bones. This is important. It tells us that these people had the ability to mentally visualize, to learn, explore, and communicate complex concepts, capturing in paint the spiritual essence of animals.

What exactly did you just see then darting across your path or in front of your car or outside your window? There are incredible creatures "out there" living with us on this planet and just because they aren't immediately in our face doesn't mean they don't hold an important position.

—*Margo McLean*

Though some might disagree, I believe that the part-human, part-animal figures they painted expressed the intuitive process of humans merging with animals as a method of learning, not as a literal manifestation.

Because the artists of the Lascaux caves are not here to tell us in their own words what they had in mind, we must borrow words of other artists and use our imaginations to speculate. I am convinced that what we find at Lascaux is evidence of a people who received spiritual inspiration and understanding through animals and the natural landscape. They saw themselves as inseparable from nature, not outside it. They learned about themselves through the teachings of the animals. Their ability to create highly expressive art tells us that they were capable of intuitive learning, which is part of every spiritual practice. It is through our intuitive capacities that we might gather clues for how animals might teach us and how we may once again remember that we are not masters of nature but only parts of it.

Discovering a Different World

Artifacts of ancient Earth-centered societies, such as we find at Lascaux, offer clues that can guide us in the modern world toward a better understanding of ourselves and our place in nature. Through ancient artifacts such as these, we can reach back to our roots, to a moment in our evolution when we still lived in awe of the Mystery. These ancient artifacts and the humble appreciation of the Earth's gifts which many indigenous people still honor today may help to reunite us with the natural world. Maybe then, we will do better when we are called to choose between the ecstasy of connecting with spirit and the exploitation of each other and our natural resources.

It is all too easy to sentimentalize a *return to nature,* to see it as a simpler way of life, which in most ways it is not. We have to take a giant step beyond mere sentiment, to see nature not as an escape from the complexity of our lives, but as a search for solutions. In facing our present global problems, this kind of spiritual knowledge becomes a key to our survival. Some solutions will come from modern technology, I am sure. But I am just as sure that the guidance to lead us beyond technology must come from the indigenous cultures which know how to learn from the animals and which honor our place within nature. Our problems today are not mechanical but spiritual. Early spiritual practices hold secrets for finding our way back to a more reverent and harmonious relationship with our planet and each other.

Nature-based spiritual practices such as I describe here do not preach the doctrine of "manifest destiny," placing man above all other life forms on our planet. They start from the premise that we are all connected—that from the tiniest virus to the most powerful creature on Earth, we are joined—and that what happens to one of us happens to all.

Capturing the Spirit of the Hunt

As I study photos of the Lascaux paintings, I ask why they found the hunt to be a theme worthy of such deep contemplation and artistic effort. What lessons did these people find in hunting, so profound that they were inspired to invest such vast time and energy? Black Elk asserted that hunting is "life's quest for ultimate truth (Smith 1991)." This might well be the case, for if they were only interested in providing meat for their families, wouldn't the Cro-Magnons have better invested their time creating more efficient weapons?

We all start out in this world as tiny seeds—no different from our animal brothers and sisters, the deer, the bear, the buffalo, or the trees, the flowers, the winged people. Every particle of our bodies comes from the good things Mother Earth has put forth.

—Ed McGaa, Eagle Man

Ironically, hunting was probably one of the first things humans learned from animals, as they observed the sacrifice of one life form for the survival of another. The mountain lion or other great cat, whose ghostly presence haunts the paintings, took down the bison calf to feed its own family. And so it is here, at the point when humans first experience the deliberate taking of a life, that we encounter the greatest mystery of all—the mystery of life and death as an integral part of an endless cycle, driven by invisible forces which are a challenge for human intellect to grasp. It is in the hunt that our ancestors would have observed the spirit leaving the body, departing forever from its physical form.

Judging from the emotion expressed in their paintings, I have no doubt that Cro-Magnon people, eight to twelve thousand years ago, struggled with the grief and pain of death and dying, but not without an awareness of how the sacrifice of an animal provided the hunter and his family with meat to nourish them and furs to warm them during long, frigid nights. And when one of his own family members or a tribal member died, Cro-Magnon could not escape the awareness that the cycle of birth and death was something shared by all life forms, large and small—from the humblest spider to deer, oxen, and humans. These lessons came about as a by-product of man's relationship to the animals, and almost certainly caused him to wonder about the spiritual bond they shared.

The beauty and grace of the paintings at Lascaux convince me that Cro-Magnons had a human sensitivity very close to our own; that is, an awareness of what we call heart or soul, an awareness of a spiritual essence that every life form verified. Like us they grieved, loved, had an appreciation for the beauty of creation, which they expressed most eloquently through their exquisite paintings of animals. They were moved by birth and death, events which filled them with awe, and they found this sense of awe in the hunt, in the sacrifice of one divine and beautiful creation for the survival of another.

Life lived in the presence of birth and death fosters an awareness of how fragile, vulnerable, and infinitely mysterious individual life really is. Yet, new life continues to sprout forth, pointing to the presence of an invisible force that itself appears to be eternal and larger than the Universe itself. The ancient hunters might have even felt the need to respect a balance between what they took and what the natural flow from the Supreme Source could provide. For the indigenous peoples of the world, for as far back in history as we can reach, hunting and gathering of Earth's bounty were spiritual encounters in their own right, not lightly taken. Rituals honoring the process were performed before and after the fact, and these might well have been the basis for all early religions.

Blessing the Prey

John Matthews has spent nearly four decades studying the Western mystery traditions and is acknowledged internationally for his work. He has noted that shamans mediate

between the seen and unseen worlds. In some traditions, the hunter performs rituals that suggest he does the same, perhaps acting as the representative of the shaman. In the following, Matthews reflects on the spiritual responsibilities of the early hunters:

"Thus, the glorious cave paintings at Lascaux . . . depicting men in the act of hunting and killing a variety of creatures, not only represent the magical aspects of the hunt, but also the shaman's dream-magic, performed before the hunt sets forth. In this, the hunter (or his representative) entered into a symbiotic relationship with the beast in order to anticipate its every action and, perhaps more importantly, to make contact with its spirit-self in order to explain the need of the tribe for its flesh and fur (Matthews 1991)."

I myself have spent considerable time studying the Zuni culture of New Mexico. Their stories tell of elaborate rituals conducted before, during, and after hunts, verifying John Matthews' observations. A hunter begins his quest for game through prayerful counsel with the spirits of certain totem, or fetish, animals—perhaps a mountain lion, a coyote, or a bobcat. This ritual might be performed with the assistance of small stone carvings of the animals that the hunter has chosen for his guides. In addition, the hunter might call upon the spirit of his prey, telling the animal of his intent and asking the animal's permission to use its flesh and its hide to feed and clothe his family and his people.

Once he has set out on his hunt, the hunter is in continuous spiritual contact with his prey, as well as with the spirit animals whose assistance he has requested for tracking his game. While the hunter's spirit animal—perhaps a mountain lion—counseled him on the delicate art of tracking his prey, there were other lessons to be learned as well. In observing his spirit animal the hunter would also observe that particular creature's stealth in maintaining and protecting its territory. He might see qualities in the animal that teach him how to manage relationships in his own world—such as the importance of recognizing one's own and other beings boundaries. He feels these things at a cellular level and literally begins to feel himself move and think like the mountain lion—becoming him.

At the point when the hunter spots his game and is close enough to kill his quarry, he pauses to plant a prayer stick and offer prayers for the animal's spirit to pass swiftly to the next world. That done, the hunter moves into action, making certain that his arrow or spear is quick in its mission. Even as the animal lays dying, the hunter rushes forward and cradles its head to his body. Then, pressing his lips to its mouth, he exchanges its last breaths with it. This ritual is one of literally intermingling the spirits of hunter and hunted, of honoring the sacrifice and acknowledging their spiritual bonds. Unlike modern day hunters, he joins spirits with the animal instead of separating himself from his prey.

Before the hunter's family can partake of the flesh of this sacrificed animal, they too must acknowledge its spirit by ritually repeating the exchange of breath. For them it is a prayer of thanksgiving, one that they fully acknowledge, speaking to the spiritual bonds they share and the supreme sacrifice of the animal they are preparing to eat.

In honoring the spirit of the animal, whose very existence lends support to the hunter's life, we acknowledge the manifestation of spirit in all its various forms. Without acknowledging the sacred in all that the Earth supports, the spirit of the bison or deer or other animal is abandoned, floating aimlessly in space—perhaps never to incarnate again, bringing the extinction of his kind and threatening all. We know instinctively that extinction of any species can be disastrous not only for that animal and its family, but for all those who are dependent on this animal and its kin for food, fur, and wisdom.

Early Teachings of the Animals

There can be no doubt that people who live very close to nature, sharing the same geographic space with the animals, have a special relationship with them that most of us find difficult to even imagine. Some years ago, I heard a Navajo man talking about the world of his grandfather, a hundred years ago. His grandfather described how, during certain celebrations, there would be a group of people sitting around a fire eating the meat of a deer they had roasted. Everyone kept a little club beside them to smack coyotes who would rush in and grab meat from the revelers' hands. Wiser coyotes would sit patiently, just behind a celebrant—sometimes close enough to feel the heat of their bodies, waiting to be tossed a bone. Though the coyotes were far from tame, they were always close by, apparently considering themselves members of the human pack. Being opportunists at heart, the coyotes knew a good thing when they saw it. Similarly, small children tamed baby foxes as pets.

With such a proximity between animals and humans, there was the opportunity to observe animals closely and learn from them. For example, the human hunter observed that the mountain lion was a masterful tracker, one who nearly always had success. So the human hunter watched carefully, taking this animal as a mentor. In the process, the human observed other things about this animal's ways, and through storytelling passed this information on to others in his family and community. He might tell of how the mountain lion staked out a specific territory of her own and how she protected that territory. That rigorous protection of boundaries then became a model for the humans when they had to defend their own boundaries from marauding neighbors.

> *The idea of balancing things serves a very special purpose in the Circle of Life. It is as a river of kindness that flows through the Circle with much energy. In our lives, we must not be so concerned with what we're trying to accomplish that we forget our true purpose of being helpers, or caretakers.*
>
> —*Michael Garrett*

Characteristics noticed in the animals became object lessons for the humans. For instance, in the Pomo communities in Northern California, near where I live, there was an elder known as Bear Woman. It was her duty to confront and punish offensive characters in the tribe. She was obviously well-named since her appearance, behavior, and official function in the community were very bear-like indeed. She captured the spirit of a mother bear protecting her cubs, and woe to anyone who dared to offend!

In a wilderness shared by humans and animals, the lessons of living would be referenced according to what one witnessed in the world around him or her. The often vain and arrogant behavior of coyotes, constantly repeating the same self-destructive blunders, became the object of literally thousands of stories. Many of these stories taught the dangers of acting in selfish ways, of judging the world only according to your own limited perceptions. They told about the dangers of acting out of vanity, that is, without reference to greater wisdom beyond the limits of your own life.

Coyote stories teach us that wisdom comes only when we can temper our own pride with experience and respect for sacred knowledge. If it is the coyote's fate to be trapped by his vanity, he is also a trickster, capable of luring us into situations where we must confront our own vanity. His teachings are so important because, by reverse example, he forces us to reflect on the core issue of the human condition—our seemingly infinite capacity for self-deception and arrogance.

Each species of animal has its own idiosyncratic lessons to teach. Each one's very existence causes us to reflect, and in the process of reflecting deeply we are provided with new lessons about the spiritual truths that direct our lives.

What Is Possible?

Is it possible for those of us who were born in modern cities, immersed in technology, to experience our lives in the ways we've been exploring? I am convinced not only that it is but that it is something we must do. Regardless of how

Ever since I first began to hear a hermit thrush singing out of a hillside, hidden from view, I have tried to stop, look, and listen for the qualities of things unseen.

—*John Hay*

far we have come, any illusions we have that we are separate from nature are only that—illusions.

Learning to think in a different way—one that reconnects us with nature, drawing wisdom from the beasts and the fowls as the Bible tells us—is only one aspect of our survival, but it is a critical one. Recycling aluminum cans, stopping the cutting and burning of the rain forests, and preventing the further deterioration of the atmosphere may be important, but these efforts are not enough. We must have a change of mind, a change of soul. We must start thinking *ecospiritually*.

I am of the conviction that we are not as far from the animals' teachings as we might think. Most of us still find comfort in nature, in walking a quiet beach, following a path through the forest, or watching an animal in the wild. Moreover, the wisdom to make the journey back to a nature-based spirituality is held in the consciousness of the Earth herself, waiting for us to receive it. The fact that we can still be moved by cave art thousands of years old, depicting a world we have never experienced directly, tells us that there is hope—that we can renew our spiritual bonds with the animals. We can begin this learning process with indigenous teachers who are willing to teach what they know of the ancient spiritual practices. Or we can do it through self-study, through spending more contemplative time in nature, or by joining an environmental group.

No matter who we are, we are only a few generations away from grandparents or great grandparents who viewed life through the lens of the natural world. My own case is an example. Toward the end of my mother's life, she related a story to me about her own birth. She was born in late October in a small fishing village on Lake Superior, in the Upper Peninsula of Michigan. At the time, my grandfather was in the Coast Guard, training to be a lighthouse keeper. Knowing there were no hospitals nearby, and that this was before cars became widespread, I asked Mother who had delivered her at her birth.

"Oh, it was my grandmother," she replied.

"Did she live with you?" I asked.

"No. She lived about twelve miles away. She had a small cabin in the woods."

"How did she get to your house?" I asked. "Did she have a horse?"

"No, that was a bad winter anyway. A horse could never have gotten through. She snowshoed."

Now my mind filled with images of this woman, at least in her mid-sixties at the time, snowshoeing by herself nearly twelve miles to deliver her grandchild. As I pondered this, another question occurred to me. "How did she know when to come?" After all, this was also before there were telephones in Upper Michigan.

"I don't know," Mother replied. "She knew just when to come. She was there for all four of us."

Mother explained that her grandmother always appeared as if summoned by magic any time there was a baby coming, an injury to fix, or an illness that needed her attention. And she often brought home-made remedies with her.

"She was a witch?" I asked.

"Oh, heavens no," Mother exclaimed, "Nothing of the sort! She was a Christian woman."

"I mean a folk healer. Were you ever at her house? What was it like?"

> *You say ecology. We think the words MOTHER EARTH have a deeper meaning. If we wish to survive, we must respect her. It is very late, but there is still time to revive and discover the old American Indian value of respect for Mother Earth. She is very beautiful, and already she is showing us signs that she may punish us for not respecting her.*
>
> *—Ed McGaa, Eagle Man*

"I think she did help other people," Mother reflected. "I've never thought of her that way. Her house was tiny, and she always had things hanging around to dry."

"Things like what?" I asked.

"Different kinds of vegetables and herbs I suppose. I never thought about it."

Mother paused, memory carrying her back seventy years. "I was twelve years old when she died," she said. "I loved her so much, but they wouldn't let me come to her funeral. I snuck out to a hill where nobody would see me, and I could look down at the cemetery where they were going to bury her. They carried her wooden casket to the grave. Then, when they started to lower the box into the hole I saw my grandmother's spirit rise out of the circle of people around the grave and go up into the sky." A little grin came over Mother's face as she remembered that moment. "I never told this to anyone else," she finished.

Three generations back in my own family was a woman who was enough in touch with the natural rhythms of life to know when her grandchildren were about to be born. Three generations back was a woman who knew her way around the woods, not only to brave the storm and snow-shoe twelve miles, but to know which herbs and roots to gather for which illnesses. She must have been pretty good at her craft since my mother, her two sisters, and her brother were born healthy and lived to ripe old age, surviving hard winters and illnesses that wiped out whole families.

There exist even today hundreds of thousands of people whose lives are still guided by nature, who know the roots and plants that can heal, and who honor the lessons of animals. They are there to inspire and instruct us, if we have the humility to ask. The old crafts of living with respect for nature, of seeking the spiritual wisdom of animals and plants and the Earth itself are not dead by any means. The teachings can come from modern day shaman teachers, from women and men who have dedicated their lives to such studies, and from within yourself.

The way of seeing that I describe in the pages ahead is drawn from a lifetime of experience—I'm 63 at the time of this writing. In my quest to experience a closer relationship with the Earth, I have drawn from many sources: from the genetic link with my great grandmother, from Native American teachers, from Nordic and Celtic influences, and from spirit teachers, including several animals that live in the wilderness that merges with my own consciousness. To the extent to which it has been possible, I've noted these sources and given due credit to my teachers.

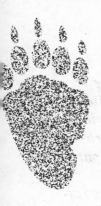

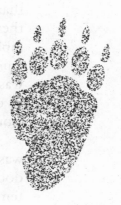

3

Seeking a Different Path

In the now long-forgotten millenniums of the paleolithic Great Hunt, where man's ubiquitous nearest neighbors were the beasts in their various species, it was those animals who were his teachers, illustrating in their manners of life the patternings of nature.

—Joseph Campbell (1972)

As a boy of sixteen, hunting near my home in rural Michigan, I spotted two rabbits and bagged them both with quick, consecutive shots from my .22 rifle. Since I was less than a half-mile from our house, I rushed home and dressed them out for dinner that night. While skinning the second rabbit, I nicked my finger, mingling my own blood with the animals'. Then, when I opened up the belly of this animal I was met by a foul smell. Deciding it must be sick, I buried its carcass in the forest. The other rabbit ended up in a delicious stew that night.

Within three days I came down with what I thought was the flu, but my fever climbed rapidly and our family doctor told my parents to rush me to the hospital. My temperature continued to escalate, so I was tucked inside a plastic body bag and packed with ice. Even so, my fever persisted and by the third day I felt totally dissociated from the physical world. That evening I had the sensation that I had little, if anything, to do with my body any more. In fact, I was certain that I had left it entirely.

My impression was that I was at least two stories above the hospital roof. I could look down through the structure into the room where my body lay, seeing everything in detail, as if I had x-ray eyes. Amazingly, I could see everything, distant or far—a capacity we all have in our dreams—but I felt wide awake and blissfully comfortable.

I stood at a crossroads, indicated by three paths of light and color. I was standing with my back to the road upon which I'd come. To my right was the road to death, and perhaps a hundred feet away was a tunnel. I was certain that once I entered this space, my life back on Earth would be finished. Though I could not see much beyond the tunnel, what I saw was a very different kind of reality, one that I can only describe as formless and invisible but definitely not Nothingness. What I sensed there moved me deeply, excited me, and part of me longed to move into it, if only to satisfy my curiosity.

To my left was a very different road. This one led back to life on Earth and to the hospital room where my body lay. As I pondered which path to take—for I was curious and excited about both of them—I could not choose. I really could not figure out how a person would make such a choice. In my youth, I suppose, I had no criteria for choosing one over the other.

> *Bringing awareness of your death into focus gives you leverage to live. It is a potent power to develop presence of mind. Plus it gives you the gumption to follow your dreams ... While using death as an advisor provides focus in your daily life, it also propels perception into non-ordinary realms.*
>
> —*Ken Eagle Feather*

At some time in the next few hours, I saw my father enter the hospital room, sit down beside my bed and take my hand. He was weeping, his head bowed. I realized he was there because the hospital had called him. I was either dying or already dead, and was not sure which it was. I thought how curious it was that anyone would cry over another person dying. I could see no reason for such grief, since death seemed harmless to me from my present vantage point.

I watched my father for some time, how long I cannot be sure. And at last, I made a decision to reenter my body—partly in deference to Dad, and partly out of curiosity about the mysterious human bond that would cause one person to grieve the death of another.

Returning to my body was easy enough. However, I was not at all sure I'd made the right choice. I now felt extremely uncomfortable, wracked with the restless ache of atrophying muscles and fever-irritated nerves that caused me to itch all over. Besides that I found I had become too weak to even turn in my bed by myself.

Not too long after returning, my fever broke and I began to feel more sensation in my arms and legs. I was no longer packed in ice, but now had blankets piled on me for warmth.

However, there were other problems that worried me even more. I could no longer see. Something had happened to my eyes. I could see light and shadow, but no color. I could not bring the ghostly figures that swam around in the world beyond my bed into sharp focus. And even though I felt the impulse to move, my muscles did not respond. I was also having some trouble with my speech.

At some point a doctor came, examined me briefly, then in a jocular tone of voice welcomed me back to the living. He explained that I had been in a "mild coma" and that, "we thought we were going to lose you there for a while." When I asked him about my sight and my difficulty moving, he was evasive.

"You apparently had tularemia," he said. "Rabbit fever."

I later discovered that this was a serious infection which people could get from rabbits. This was in the days before wide-spectrum antibiotics, which now make the disease less dangerous than it was at that time. When I had it, it was often fatal.

Upon my release from the hospital, I weighed under 110 pounds. I'd lost at least forty pounds in the five or six days I had lain in bed burning with fever. In the weeks following, my sight returned and I recovered my ability to move about. But life had changed for me. My interests had shifted. The world I saw now confused and troubled me. It was not that I felt wiser, on the contrary, I wondered if I'd suffered brain damage from the illness. I watched life going on around me as if I were on a movie set. Everyone but me knew their lines, but I could not remember even seeing the script. I felt that all this was my own failure, that I should be participating just as the others were. I not only didn't know my lines, but I had missed the beginning of the movie and could not even follow the story.

In quiet moments, I remembered being at that crossroads between life and death, looking down that long tunnel of light to a reality different from anything I had known in my everyday life. Everything had seemed so simple there, even the decision to live or die. I could not articulate all this at the time, and when I tried to tell my parents what was going on with me they stared back in silence, with a look that seemed to be asking if I was crazy. I tried to explain what I'd seen to my best friend. All I could say was that reality is not at all as we picture it in our minds. What really matters is something we can't even see or touch.

A Medicine Story

Some five years after my near-death experience I read a Winnebago medicine story from the Great Lakes area where I grew up. The story taught that the rabbit was a mythical demiurge[2] sent to Earth by the creator to help us humans come to terms with the fact that we die. The animal was charged with the duty of guiding us to the other side and then negotiating with spirits to ensure our reincarnation.

In the shamanic initiation process, the rabbit was seen as having a slightly different responsibility. Its job here was to escort the person through death to converse with the Creator and then come back to Earth to tell others what he or she had learned. I thought it interesting (at the very least) that my own journey to the edge of death and back began with a rabbit. At the time I heard this story, it occurred to me that maybe I wasn't the first person in the world to get sick from hunting and eating wild rabbits. If rabbit fever had been prevalent for a long time maybe others had experienced that other reality that I had experienced, and had been able to make sense of it. The story gave me hope that at least I wasn't losing my mind, and maybe if I pursued information about these other cultures I'd find answers to some of the questions I was beginning to ask.

You're a funny bird. You think you are going to understand by asking questions. I don't think you will, but who am I to say?

—don Juan

The Winnebago story did lead me to another way of looking at life, one that was very different than the European tradition from which I'd come. I cite the rabbit story partly because it mirrors the life-death themes illustrated in the hunt scenes at Lascaux. It also shows the universality of animals as teachers, particularly the spiritual nature of their teachings. And finally, it provides clues about the idiosyncrasies that determine the teachings of the animals, which is the key to this source of wisdom.

---

[2]Demiurge: in cosmology, one of the natural forces or helpers of creation.

Looking at rabbit's inherent characteristics, it is easy to see why the Winnebago people might have chosen this animal to represent regenerative powers such as reincarnation and returning to life from the dead. After all, the rabbit's prolific reproductive, that is, regenerative, capacities are well known, especially to farmers who are often plagued by the rabbit's mischief with their crops and granaries. The average rabbit "regenerates" at the rate of between three and six offspring per year.

I remember a conversation I had with an Ojibway elder from the Great Lakes area. We talked about animal stories, reincarnation, and how Europeans had such a different view of the afterlife than Indian peoples had. For example, the European viewed the afterlife in a very self-centered way, believing that he would go to Heaven or some place like that, with his body, ego, and personality fully intact. It was as if death was little more than a brief sleep, from which we would awaken in another place, ready to resume business as usual. It is true that the souls of great teachers live on, my Ojibway friend advised, but the Great Spirit, who is the regenerative force of the world, does not have much use for the personality part of animals—humans or otherwise—once that person's journey here on Earth is done. The good we do in this life is passed on to all beings—*two-leggeds, four-leggeds, finned, and winged people.*

The Great Spirit, my friend told me, continues to express itself, apparently without end, bringing in new humans, animals, plants, and all other life forms. That is why we are all one. While we are here on Earth, each animal and human contributes to the evolution of our planet's wisdom. We humans do much that makes no contribution at all, through deeds that we believe are profoundly important in our self-centeredness. Mostly, though, we do great destruction because we do not heed the messages that come to us from Mother Earth.

When I argued that animals can be as destructive as humans, destroying crops and even killing people, my friend shook his head and looked at me as if I were an idiot. "This happens because we are out of balance. When you take away their land, the center is lost."

Animals Are Not Symbolic

One of the most difficult things about learning from animals is to fully realize that the animals are *not symbolic*. We all have a tendency to assign meaning to this creature or that, according to something we have read in a book or learned in the course of growing up. We have fallen into the habit of assigning meaning instead of quieting our minds to listen and allow what is there to speak to us. Bound by symbolic reasoning, we think of Owl as a symbol of wisdom, Coyote as a symbol of buffoonery and trickery, and Bear as a cuddly stuffed toy, akin to our childhood teddy bears.

If not symbols, or at least archetypes, what are the animals? The most direct answer is that they are who they are—living, breathing creatures who have their own personalities and their own patterns of behavior. And it is from our observation of these behaviors that we learn to connect with, and learn from, the natural world.

In the Zuni cosmology, as reported by Frank Hamilton Cushing, an intuitive anthropologist who lived with the Zunis for several years in the late 1800s, the world we know today emerged out of formlessness. How it did this, of course, is the great unsolvable mystery of our existence. The Zuni people, however, believe that the formlessness out of which our world emerged now expresses itself in an infinite number of ways, in forms as wide-ranging as lighter-than-air gases to great mountain ranges. Animal and human forms also manifest in numerous ways. For example, *wolfness* is manifest in the animal we call wolf. But it is also manifest in human actions, in the shapes of certain rocks, and in numerous other ways.

All of these manifestations, in both the physical and spiritual worlds, are constantly in transition. Just as the tiny seed becomes a stalk of corn with many ears, so the form of an animal comes from the joining of male and female seeds.

So, too, do the actions and character of an animal, person, or a natural phenomenon transform and reappear in other forms—from rock formations to human thoughts. The circle of form, to formlessness, and back to form is eternal.

The infinite manifestations we experience in the world, taken collectively, express the creating spirit, and are the source of our oneness. Cushing believed that the Zunis, more than any other peoples he knew of, were on the right track. Out of their cosmology and religion we might one day discover the prototypes for every motion of the human soul. Because so much of the Zunis' way of life came from observing the animals, it seemed logical to Cushing that he might discover these spiritual prototypes in the animals.

In traditional stories, in totemism, and in animal fetishism, the teachings of one animal or another only come to us by carefully observing the animals in their natural environment. To do this, we must empty our minds and think of them as expressions of spirit, that is, as manifestations of form out of formlessness. People who live this way ask very different kinds of questions than, say, the scientist who is primarily seeking ways to quantify cause and effect. The person living in the natural environment prior to the technological age is asking questions such as: "What is spirit expressing through this animal?" "What is this animal all about?" If we pay attention, maybe we will find answers to come to a

The animals—the winged and even the small crawling ones—remind us that we are all related, all part of the created whole. When we observe nature, our egos can be dispelled, and we learn to make our requests in humility and need. The great vastness projects its immensity and lets us know that we are but a tiny speck in vast, indescribable, ultimate space. That alone teaches us humility and brings us down to size.

—*Ed McGaa, Eagle Man*

deeper understanding of our own spiritual nature, and our relationship to the planet.

While the spiritual lessons are profound, there is also much practical wisdom that comes by observing animals. As we noted in chapter two, Cro-Magnon man probably learned how to hunt by watching animals. But we don't have to look even that far to see examples of the animals' practical teachings. In the American Southwest a hundred and fifty years ago, a hunter might have watched a mountain lion hunting, seen the stealth with which she moved as she tracked an animal, noticed how she kept downwind of her prey so as not to be detected by scent, and then saw how she quietly moved closer and closer until she was near enough to pounce and make a clean kill. There was a craft to learn, and while Mountain Lion instinctively followed that craft, humans had to learn it by example.

If they were asking questions such as, "What is spirit expressing with this animal?" it is easy to imagine that a person living in an environment teeming with rabbits would see them as revealing spirit's great regenerative powers. From the perspective of farmers, whose crops are ruined by rabbits, this prolific animal must seem like an absolute master of regeneration, with at least three new rabbits turning up for every one that dies. (Much to the farmer's dismay, I might add.)

In Northern Michigan, the rabbit is not only seen by native people as an expert on regeneration, and as a guardian on the passage from life to death, it is also seen as having transformative powers. This notion also comes from observing the animal in nature. In snowy regions it changes color with the seasons, from dusty brown in the summer to white in the winter. By blending with the underbrush in the summer and snow in the winter, rabbits make themselves less vulnerable to predation by other animals such as the hawk, the fox, or the dog.

Rabbit teaches us that we don't necessarily need superior weapons to protect ourselves against animals, or humans, or even natural elements which might harm us. The lesson we learn is that we can also make ourselves invisible to them or run for cover.

In ancient Celtic legends, Rabbit sits with Raven, assisting Taliesin, the Bardic Shaman of the British Isles. Writers around the sixth century told of Taliesin's ability to change himself into any animal, and it was presumably through these spirit guardians, Raven and Rabbit, that he gained such powers.

The rabbit's timidity also appears in myths, with his shyness and fear often getting him into trouble. At the very least, these lessons are dire warnings of what it means to hold back and be afraid to speak up for ourselves. At best, Rabbit teaches us that in order to survive as timid creatures, we must, like Rabbit, use our cleverness to evade threats to our well-being.

> *Nearness to nature ... keeps the spirit sensitive to impressions not commonly felt, and in touch with the unseen powers.*
>
> —*Ohiyesa*

Recognizing Spirit's Gifts

Over the years, my perception of my nearly fatal encounter with Rabbit has gone through many revisions. At first, I saw this creature as a scourge, a carrier of disease, one that had nearly killed me (never mind that it was I who killed the rabbit). As I struggled to come to terms with my near-death experience, I also began to see my rabbit as an instrument of my fate. Why, I began to ask, had this experience of becoming ill and encountering death fallen to me? What could I do with this experience to bring it into a more positive focus?

Eight years following that difficult winter, I met and began working with a peyote teacher who taught me how to look at the rabbit in a completely different way. It turned out that this teacher was a shaman, though I wasn't familiar with that word at the time, and did not even recognize that he was from a very different cultural background than I. He introduced me to peyote, and during the two years of our association—filled with challenges and dangers—I came to appreciate the rabbit in a new way. I no longer saw it as my foe, but as an almost magical ally and guardian who taught me as much as the peyote was teaching, stripping away my illusions. Through Rabbit I had come to the beginning of a path that I might never have found in any other way. It had introduced me to the invisible reality, the reality of inexorable emotion, dreams, and spiritual revelation that determine the courses of our lives.

Today I wear a small medicine pouch around my neck. Inside, along with other objects, is a small silver figure of a rabbit. The rabbit fetish reminds me to give thanks to this animal, who has become an important guide and teacher for a very different kind of path. This animal has become what some call a "power animal" for me. This little talisman near my heart reminds me of Rabbit's blessings. I must confess, however, that nearly thirty years passed before I could see Rabbit in this positive light and begin integrating what it has shown me and what would become an essential aspect of my personal voice.

Spirit Animals, Symbolism, and the Power of the Story

In Frank Rivers' wonderful little book, *The Way of the Owl* (1997), he talks about this bird's natural qualities and suggests that it is an excellent model for our own behavior. He says:

> The owl is acutely aware and adaptive. He routinely varies his behavior and defensive strategies to adjust to changing conditions. He is flexible in his feeding habits and nest-building choices. He varies his territories to fit food supplies and population densities. His vision and hearing are outstanding. In this, the owl makes a perfect model for mastery. Owls have much to teach us about living in a conflicted and ever-changing world.

The person, then, who observes and models her own behavior after what she finds in the owl, could develop a wide repertoire of skills, giving her great versatility. She could become a master of sensitivity, with marvelous physical presence. Neither aggressor nor victim, hers would be a third path between eagle and dove. She would be as adept at fighting as not-fighting, and even though she can defend herself, she is always ready to negotiate if the opportunity arises.

Each and every animal is one way that the creating spirit is manifest, giving it (spirit) expression, and thus offering us a literal universe of possibilities. Every animal, ourselves included, has been given its own individuality, with gifts and character and special challenges unique to it. Together, in the endless circle of life, they collectively give the creating spirit a voice—a voice like a huge chorus made up of all that the Universe holds. By observing even a small circle of life as creation's voice, we not only gain much wisdom about the animals, we gain wisdom about how we might shape our own lives to be in concert with Creation's plan.

We know from genetics that diversity provides for the possibility of a population coping with a wide spectrum of environmental changes. That diversity is the foundation for its ability to *survive* change. The vast gene pool that spirit offers on our planet has allowed new variations of plants, animals, insects, fishes, and even humans to evolve, having survived many drastic changes. This same diversity, and each creature's ability to learn from the others has accounted for the survival of the life force itself on this planet, even under dire conditions.

In the same way that diversity of living beings has ensured that we have a healthy gene pool, diversity of behavior and understanding ensure an expanding, increasingly creative collective consciousness. Animals provide diversity not only in substance but in form—in the way we think and act. Imagine, if you will, that we could join every living thing on planet Earth at a vast circle, and out of this

circle that a single collective voice could arise. This single voice would be that of Creation, which sings every day. We need only find the ears to listen. The animals hear it always.

Where to Start

To begin any new endeavor, most of us seek a foundation in tradition; that is, by looking at what already exists. If we are learning an art, we may start by looking at, and maybe even copying, the work of artists we admire. In time, we may develop our own way of working and moving beyond our teachers, altering what we've learned from them so that with much practice it becomes our own. Building upon tradition, that is, upon what is already known and has stood the test of time, is essential. At the same time it is important to examine tradition and make certain it still serves.

The work I presently do with spirit animals started with a combination of spiritual practices, drawn from many sources: from indigenous cultures of the Great Lakes area where I grew up, from the Zuni people of New Mexico, from my readings of Celtic lore, and from African medicine stories. Even as a child of seven, I collected totems and talismans of animals. My collection included a miniature of an Eskimo totem pole and several miniature figures of animals I admired. I also had the classic Chinese figure of three monkeys: hear no evil, see no evil, speak no evil. Bats fascinated me, their flickering flights directed by sonar carried my imagination to the secrets of the night world.

For me, animals possessed a grace that humans lacked. Even when I was very young, I would watch them in the woods near our home and try to understand what exactly it meant to have this kind of grace. I was not yet familiar with the religious idea of grace, of being sanctified because we are living in full accord with God's plan. But that is how it seemed to me, that the animals did not spend quite so much time as we humans do privately composing the meaning and purpose of our lives. It was the animals' lack of self-consciousness that attracted me. They lived as if they were completely in tune with a larger plan, and I longed to know that plan as they apparently did.

At night I would hold an animal talisman in my hand and imagine myself being that animal. It was a kind of meditation, though I did not know what that meant at the time. In my mind's eye I would become that creature, feeling what it might be like to trot through the forests on all fours or have my life directed by the invisible cues that animals apparently received.

Recalling those early years of my life, I can imagine that this practice was not so different from what our paleolithic cousins must have done. The animals surrounding them, far outnumbering the people, must have seemed like mysterious dancers, choreographed by an invisible guiding force which they dared not even name. Somehow, the very existence of the animals was evidence enough of the mystery they had not yet named or tried to rationalize. In their efforts to understand this mystery, they painted pictures of the animals. Perhaps performing dances like theirs, watching intently until their dances flowed through their consciousness as vitally as they flowed across the open plains. In the caves at Lascaux, they stopped time, the paintings allowing them to hold the imagery still, long enough to bask in the awe of it and perhaps draw a little closer to the Source.

And so it is with us, as we seek to receive whatever truths the animals might offer us about our lives.

A New Developmental Perspective

Developmental psychology is the study of what we must learn at each step on our way to maturity. Indigenous cultures draw their models from observing how people relate to the natural world, and the path of development they prescribe is usually based on living in harmony with nature. They recognize their interdependence with the planet, and so they look at how they can protect that which nurtures them. By contrast, mainstream psychology has

been based almost exclusively on values invented by other humans and on our development within a single species—our own—as if we were the only species populating the planet.

At best, our modern developmental systems ignore the possibility that the kinds of relationships we establish with the co-inhabitants of our planet might have an impact on the quality of all our lives. Surely the way we relate to Mother Earth and the other creatures living here deserves as much attention as how we relate to the women from whose bodies we came or the father who fertilized the egg, or how well prepared we are going to be to make a lot of money.

Well-being occurs when we seek and find our unique place in the Universe and experience the continuous cycle of receiving and giving through respect and reverence for the beauty of all living things.

—*Michael Garrett*

Though I hold a doctorate in psychology, I feel this discipline has done us a great disservice in terms of our relationship with the Earth—and it may have even contributed to the environmental crisis we face today. At the very least, mainstream psychology ignores the possibility that the kinds of relationships we establish with the co-inhabitants of the Earth might have an impact on the quality of our own lives.

Transpersonal psychology adds spiritual development to healthy ego development, which is a step in the right direction, but even this approach pays only meager attention to ecospiritual concerns such as our internal perceptions of other species and what our relationships with them should be if we are to sustain a healthy biosphere. It seems strange to me that modern psychology could overlook an area of such vital concern, one that indigenous peoples have not only known about for thousands of years, but have made central to their cultures. It just might be that, were we to truly appreciate the roles that all our diverse species play in the universal plan, we would never have been capable of the exploitation of nature that is the root of the environmental problems we face today. If modern psychology is to truly serve as the "science of human nature," it needs to vastly broaden its perspective.

One of my spirit teachers, Awahakeewah, speaks of the wholeness of human development as "finding the center." Twenty years ago he advised, "To find the center and live in balance, you've got to jump out of your skin . . . look at the world through the clear eyes of soaring Eagle and the blind eyes of burrowing Mole." He was referring, of course, to what we must do to seek the wisdom of the animals.

The great wisdom that the Native Americans and other indigenous peoples offer us focuses on the intimate spiritual connections we need to develop with all of existence, from the seemingly most meager grain of sand, to our animal and plant brothers and sisters, to Mother Earth and Father Sky, and to the Infinite. Until we incorporate these into our personal development, we live as aliens on the Earth. And don't fool yourself, we feel that alienation acutely, though we have devised ways to desensitize ourselves to the feelings of homelessness it fosters. Feeling alienated from the Earth, we numb ourselves with excesses and addictions aimed at avoiding this dull pain that we cannot even identify. Our first step may be to admit that we have spent several thousand years deepening our alienation from the Earth rather than healing it.

Kenny Ausubel speaks of a "global renaissance, at the heart of which is the simple principle of reverence for life in all its forms . . . founded on a new covenant with nature and a reaffirmation of compassion for all the world's peoples." He speaks of people from a "wide spectrum of faiths who are calling for us to reintegrate ourselves as benign stewards within the web of life while honoring the sacredness of the Earth. The teachings of many indigenous peoples inspire us to remember that the Earth is alive and that all life is sacred (1997)."

The Ecospiritual Wheel, described in the following chapter, presents seven developmental cycles aimed at the integration process Ausubel calls for. The spirit animals who come to this wheel bring teachings which weave together the seen and unseen worlds into a developmental process that places each of us into the web of life, spiritually aligning us with the Earth.

4

The Ecospiritual Wheel

"All created things are alive, conscious, and want to communicate. The Creator has endowed all creatures with wisdom and joy, and they are eager to share with us their ways of being in the world. In time we learn to recognize them as our companions."

—Tom Cowan (1996)

The Ecospiritual Wheel is the first Wheel of Life teaching that I was given. It is aimed at deepening our awareness of our spiritual interdependence with all life on the planet. Through seven animal teachers, this wheel identifies personal developmental cycles which each of us must complete if we are to find our place within the web of life.

On a personal level, this wheel helps us identify those cycles that we have completed and points us in the direction to complete the ones we still need to work on. We experience the benefits of this work in feelings of coming to our center. We find the gifts through which we can serve our home here on the Earth, and which will give our lives new direction and meaning.

As we work with this wheel, we may experience vague feelings of alienation and discomfort, which are normal in any process of personal growth. The good news is that the alienation dissolves in the light of new revelations that emerge from the animals' teachings. Out of the work at this wheel will come a greater capacity to make choices and decisions from an ecospirtual perspective, honoring all of life.

Each of the seven developmental cycles is based on the principle of looking through the clear eyes of soaring Eagle and the blind eyes of burrowing Mole. You will see how this works as we go along. You might note, by the way, that while Eagle and Mole are participants in this circle, there are five other animals as well. As you proceed, it will become apparent to you why each animal was chosen for the particular developmental cycle to which it is assigned.

The root concept is that to live on the Earth, we need to learn what it means to live in harmony with the higher order of the planet itself. For example, though we may be spiritual beings, we are taking a physical form. As such, we need to come to terms with some very basic facts, such as the care of that physical form. If we walk out in front of a thirty-ton truck, bearing down on us at seventy miles per hour, chances are pretty good that we are going to complete our Earth journey prematurely. That's a very basic lesson that we learn early on—that the physical body that hosts our spirit is not indestructible. In fact, that issue, our mortality, will continue to be an overriding theme throughout our lives.

Our physical form remains healthy and intact only through the charity of Mother Earth, and can be ensured only as long as Her health is ensured. From Her breast we receive nutrients, and from the atmosphere She maintains we receive oxygen. From Her rivers and oceans we receive the vital fluids our physical forms require. Hopefully, we would learn that the loving care She extends to us must be reciprocated. Our physical forms also have basic needs such as cleanliness, and even subtler issues such as respecting the boundaries between ourselves and other beings—from microbes to the beasts of the jungle. We must also learn to recognize others of our own species who don't have our best interests at heart, be it an angry ex-lover, another

Figure 4.1. The Ecospiritual Wheel

nation, or a mega-corporation whose own self-interests result in actions that threaten the entire biosphere.

But all of these come back to the matter of how we relate to Mother Earth. Would we abuse Her in the name of growing our food? Protecting ourselves from microbes? From animals? From others of our own species who would do us harm? Would we abuse Her if there was enough money in it for us? So far, you have probably noted by now, we have done all of these and more with little concern for Mother Earth's well-being.

All these issues are important to our development and survival if we are to live on the Earth in the twenty-first century. All the concepts I've mentioned thus far are obvious, dealing primarily with maintaining the integrity of our physical bodies. Beyond these, however, are more complex issues, such as those which arise when we ask what constitutes real quality of life. What do we need to develop if we are to honor the Creating Spirit's plan? It apparently includes the concept of a continuum, that is, of a self-sustaining and self-regenerating biosphere. How shall we balance our own physical and emotional needs with those of the other creatures with whom we share this world?

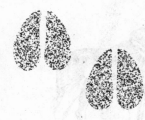

For anyone reading this book there may also be highly individualized and personal developmental questions. For example, you might ask, what is missing in my development? Which cycles are incomplete? What must I do to feel at home in this lifetime? How do I make new choices which will better reflect the person I would like to be? What changes in which developmental cycles, could improve my relationships with others, with the environment, with a higher power, with myself?

Human history has demonstrated that positive change comes about when deep personal promptings motivate individuals to act collectively. This kind of motivation comes from our souls, and from a conviction that is built on something more than faith or reason. By experiencing our connection with the Creating Spirit, which is the aim of the animals' teachings, we perhaps may come into greater alignment with our Creator's intent. And this is where we find the kind of motivation we need to bring greater love into our relationships with Mother Earth, to bring about the kinds of change needed to save our planet.

Transformation takes place one person at a time, so it is

vital that each person tend to his or her own development. The collective effort always includes both those who gather in numbers and those who stand alone holding the power. Both are necessary.

You will notice that the animals who sit at the Ecospiritual Wheel (page 47) have a wide range of physical relationships to the Earth; from Mole who lives closest to the Earth's center, literally under her skin, to Eagle who lives furthest from it and closest to the sky. Badger scratches and digs around on the surface of the Earth, belly mostly pressed to the ground. Wolf is four-legged and fast, racing over her surface. Bear ambles about on all fours, but rises on two legs when it serves her to do so. Mountain Lion, with strength and speed superior to most other animals, almost seems to fly as her powerful leaps propel her over impossible terrain. Eagle, of course, reigns supreme of all birds in the sky.

There is one more—the power animal—an unknown in this Wheel, since each person who sits here will have his or her own animal (I will discuss how to meet your own power animal in a later chapter). Together, these seven will assist us on our journey to wholeness. Each one will guide us along its own path, with all paths leading back to our common source, the Earth. Here is the purpose of this developmental model, to bring a guidance system into our lives that will get us back on track with the spiritual forces of our planet.

It is my understanding that in the Zuni religion, humans are believed to be the most finished of animals, yet the furthest from the highest source. (They have no word for God or the Creating Source, believing it presumptuous of humans, with their perceptual limitations, to provide a name.) Our own free will, which as far as we know makes us unique among animals, gives us the ability to believe we know more than we are actually capable of knowing. Some say it is our free will that got us kicked out of the Garden of Eden—that having eaten from the tree of knowledge, we presumed to know as much as God. So God, like the parent of ungrateful children, said, "Well, okay. You think you know it all, go out into the bigger world and see how you do!" But we made a mistake.

What we took for perfect knowledge was not that, but only the ability to create our own perceptions of the world. While this is a wonderful gift God bestowed upon us, it leaves us with a lot of room for error—mainly, we create perceptions that are not accurate. These perceptions generate dualities, illusions of being separate from the Universe because the one out there does not conform to the one in our heads. Having divorced ourselves—or having been divorced—from our source, we require the help of our animal mediators to get back on track.

While we struggle with free will and human perception, the other animals in the web of life go along guided by what we call "instinct." They follow a guidance system for their lives that keeps them always connected with their Source. They experience no dualities. The animals, being closest to this source, can mediate for us, assisting us in finding our way to the center—but only if we are willing to take the time to listen to them. I have always liked this concept. A woman in a workshop some years ago said that, for her, each animal at the wheel becomes like a separate prayer through which she could find her wholeness and feel a very personal connection with that which she could not name.

Each With a Message

You may find it easier to picture the animal teachers and their developmental lessons in the table on page 60, which I call "Developmental Cycles of Life." Later, we will reassemble the spirit animals at the wheel. For now, the table organizes the animals in a linear way—which of course does not actually occur in Nature—making it easier to track the developmental processes of our journey here on Earth.

Mole

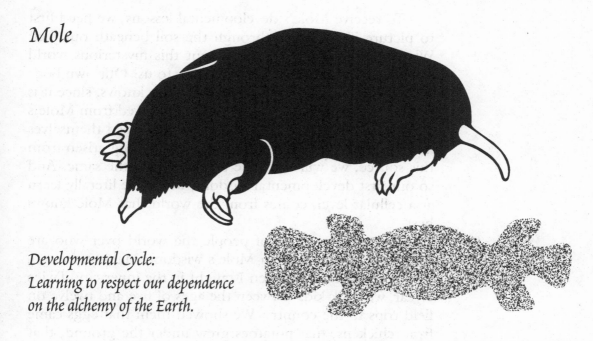

Developmental Cycle:
Learning to respect our dependence
on the alchemy of the Earth.

Long ago, it is said, Mole chose to live within Mother Earth, never leaving her womb except for brief forays to the surface. Mole, more than all animals, has thus come to know the alchemy of the Earth, the chemistry of the soil, and the relationships between all the life forms: roots of plants, grubs, worms, and microorganisms that share her home with it. Mole knows what goes on under the Earth's skin to produce what we see from the ground above.

Some say that our relationship with Mole starts at the moment of our conception, since the minerals and nutrients that make our own lives possible come from the Earth. When we assume our physical form, we also assume a dependence on all that is born out of the Earth's womb. It is, after all, from this place that all the building blocks of life come. Even the milk that we suckle at our mother's breast, or that we receive from a cow or goat, is made from the bounty that our planet provides.

To receive Mole's developmental lessons, we need first to picture it tunneling through the soil beneath our feet. What does this animal know about this mysterious world that is so familiar to her, so unfamiliar to us? Our own bodies are already attuned to some of what it knows, since it is out of the nutrients that our mothers received from Mole's world that cells formed, divided and organized themselves into the physical body we now inhabit. Having arisen from this source, we will continue to grow from the same. And so our first developmental wisdom, which we literally learn at a cellular level, comes from the world that Mole knows best.

There are millions of people the world over who are spiritually separated from Mole's wisdom. Many years ago, I saw this in children when I taught in the inner city. Twice a year, we took kids between the ages of five and twelve on field trips to the country. We showed them that eggs came from chickens, that potatoes grew under the ground, that apples came from trees, and that hamburgers came from cows who fed on the grass, then were slaughtered and ground up for sandwiches. Mostly, these kids were incredulous, denying what their eyes were telling them. Some swore they would never eat eggs or chicken or hamburger again, and didn't touch these foods for several days. In the end, of course, they went back to old food habits—except for one or two who actually became vegetarians.

These kids talked about their trip to the country for days, sometimes weeks. It changed how they thought about what they put in their bodies. Hopefully, it changed how a few of them thought about Mother Earth Herself.

But inner-city kids are not the only ones who somehow missed this developmental cycle or were otherwise severed from the wisdom of Mole. It is difficult to imagine that chemical companies who produce fertilizers and pesticides which saturate Mother Earth's flesh, and surely threaten Mole's well-being, have learned the lessons of this developmental cycle.

To enhance your development within this cycle, sense the world of Mole through mole-eyes. Imagine yourself being able to project your consciousness into its world. Make up stories to tell yourself about Mole's discoveries in the world beneath our feet. Even play with the idea of imagining every cell of your being sharing this special subterranean wisdom, the alchemical link between yourself and Mother Earth's womb.

For a day or two, carry on imaginary conversations with Mole, picking its brain to find out how the cells that now make up your physical presence arose from the alchemy of the soil that this animal knows so well.

Badger

Developmental Cycle: Recognition of individual needs, care of self as a separate physical entity.

Observing Badger in the wild, you'd find an extremely aggressive animal. Built close to the ground, he rests his muscular belly on the soil as he digs furiously in search of roots, rodents, or grubs upon which he might dine. Its long, sharp claws, similar to a bear's, are particularly suited for digging, which he does extremely well.

With hair-trigger reflexes, he reacts to any threat to his food source or his body, acting with murderous intent, bolstered by his powerful, razor-sharp claws. Badger's behavior is the essence of the survival instincts—focused on the protection of his own physical form and on maintaining his separate well-being.

Badger energy might be compared to the energy of that part of us which acknowledges our vulnerability when we take a physical form. It is the part which recognizes that our physical form demands the satisfaction of basic nutrients and psychophysiological needs, as well as protection of the physical body itself.

The central issue of this developmental cycle is our recognition of the drive for survival as integral to the life force itself. As such, this essential drive is sacred, suggesting, at the very least, that the Creating Spirit has a purpose to be fulfilled by our taking a physical form. Because of its particular behavior and characteristics, Badger's way of being epitomizes this drive. Its singular focus on the preservation and well-being of the self provides us with a model for recognizing our responsibility to ourselves, that there is value in caring for our physical being and not separating it from the spiritual.

Once you have developed an image of Badger in your mind, refer to it whenever your energy or drive is low in your life: in health, in personal expression, in achieving a personal goal, or in any interpersonal conflicts.

Bear

Developmental Cycle: Self-knowledge and growth; standing in your own power; transition and change through the power of introspection.

In nature, we are first impressed by Bear's tremendous strength and ability to stand in its own power as few creatures do—so firmly grounded it sometimes seems to be fused with it. In the winter, Bear retreats to hibernate, minimizing the energy that would be spent dealing with the external world.

In many Earth-based spiritual societies, Bear is seen as having great powers to bring about change, making difficult transitions through the process of "hibernation." One must have great strength to do this, however, and Bear has it in abundance. Whereas the wolf's strength is in the power of the pack working together (see below), Bear's strength is in its ability to stand alone in its own power. The bear cycle includes gaining wisdom through solitude. By standing in our own power, introspection, and self-examination, we are able to effect change and transformation, since it is through these activities that we freshen the inner perspectives which might otherwise limit us.

Wolf

Developmental Cycle: Love for others; community awareness; recognition of self in relation to others.

Observed in its natural habitat, Wolf is a social animal, with powerful familial patterns of behavior. Males bond with their mates and their pups, and take part in feeding, protecting, and teaching their offspring. The individual animals instinctively hunt as a community, or pack, and share in the spoils of the hunt.

Wolves in the wild display a high level of community and family loyalty and interaction. In a healthy pack, there is also a sense of play, with both pups and mature animals taking part.

In these ways, Wolf's behavior becomes a model for the development of family and community behavior—the ability to recognize the interdependence of all members and to work constructively with others. Matters of loyalty, collaboration, and mutual trust and understanding are the teachings we assimilate in this developmental cycle. For Wolf, this sense of loyalty, community, and love extends to Mother Earth Herself.

It is important to note that if we are to function well in this cycle of our development, we must also have completed, to some degree, the lessons of Mole, Badger, and Bear. The lone wolf, who lives outside the pack but is still loosely affiliated with it, is usually one who has not fully developed its individuality (the Badger cycle) and so is too threatened or too self-centered to function in a mutually supportive way within the community. Similarly, a basic recognition of the cycle represented by Mole, with an appreciation for the alchemy of the Earth, could mean it lacked respect for essential sources—for example, killing for sport rather than biological need.

Focus on Wolf for lessons about family, community, cooperative efforts of any kind, and for balancing your individual needs against others' requirements.

Learning to stand in our own power, employing all of Wolf's gifts, in addition to integrating the lessons of Mole, Badger, and Bear, prepares us for finding and learning how to use our own voice, which is the next developmental cycle.

Power Animal

Developmental Cycle: Finding your own voice; discovering how to best use your gifts; learning to distinguish between self-power, power over others, or others' power over you.

In many shamanic cultures, the young man was sent out on a vision quest in search of his power animal, or spiritual ally. After days of fasting and enduring the hardship of being alone in the wilderness, a spiritual ally in the form of an animal would appear to him. Sometimes this animal came in a dream or vision, sometimes in the appearance of an actual animal. Sometimes they did not appear even after many vision quests but then would appear unexpectedly in an everyday situation. Through this animal, the person would then find their own power, their own gift—or as some expressed it, their own voice.

Because it is so highly individualized, the power animal may turn out to be a creature as seemingly humble as a hummingbird or as formidable as a lion. The idea of "power" in this case is not based on size or physical strength but on how the creature serves to put you in touch with your own gifts—the best of who you are and what you bring to the world.

We will be talking more about the power animal in subsequent chapters. For now, it is enough to know that it is a teacher and ally in the development of your individualized gifts and in guiding you toward their best use.

Figure 4:2
Developmental
Cycles of Life
If you are familiar with the chakras of Hindu wisdom, and what the chakras reveal about the lessons from our stay here on Earth, you may be interested to see the parallels between those teachings and the Spirit Animal* teachings. Since they are universal, these same teachings appear in diverse cultures throughout the world and in all times.

CHAKRA: CROWN
ANIMAL: EAGLE

Ability to see the Big Picture, in this case the balance between Earth beings and spirit; awareness of how our journey on Earth is not separate from our spiritual identity.

BROW
MOUNTAIN LION

Quest for wisdom; ability to differentiate between human knowledge and universal truth. Openness to the lessons of true elders, recognizing forces and truths that govern our lives and all others.

THROAT
PERSONAL POWER ANIMAL

Finding your own voice: discovering how to best use your personal gifts; learning to distinguish between self-power, power over others, or others' power over you. Honoring your gift with courage.

HEART
WOLF

Development of ability to love and care for others; community awareness and awareness of relationship; joy in nurturing and supporting others, and receiving the same for yourself to achieve all of the above.

SOLAR PLEXUS
BEAR

Self-knowledge and growth; standing in your own power; transition and change through the power of introspection; recognizing the limits of human knowing, power of humility and forgiveness.

HARA
BADGER

Recognition of individual needs, care of self as separate physical entity. The power and vulnerability of the Life Force manifest within us, acknowledging its sacredness; healing energy for self and others.

BASE
MOLE

Learning to respect our dependence on the alchemy of the Earth. First awareness of physical form, relationship to Earth, honoring the Source, respecting the alchemy of the soil that supports all life.

* Descriptions of animals and places at the wheel adapted from Zuni (New Mexico) teachings.

Mountain Lion

Developmental Cycle: Quest for wisdom (tracking); ability to differentiate between perceptual knowledge and universal knowledge/truth.

Mountain Lion is the master hunter. Watching this animal in nature we discover that it is truly tenacious in its resolve once it sets out in pursuit of its prey. There are stories of ancient hunters who were tutored by Mountain Lion to track other animals through their spoor—their footprints, droppings, and even their scent. Mountain Lion's stealth, strength, and swiftness also guarantee its success in the final kill. The values of the tenacious hunter include great wisdom as well, and so it is that through this combination of skill, wisdom, and experience this animal gains its

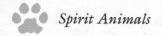
reputation for mastery. It is also confidently territorial, providing humans with clear models for setting boundaries and being clear about respecting others' processes.

This cycle of development focuses on the search for truth—that is, on the ability to discern and hopefully be guided by powers higher than our own opinions and biases. The completion of this cycle almost certainly depends upon completing, or at least profoundly understanding, the first five developmental cycles. The person achieving this level of development might well become a leader, providing counsel to individuals as well as the community.

Mountain Lion's wisdom rises out of its profound understanding and connection with the Earth and the unseen reality. It easily recognizes the truths beyond the illusions of human perception, the truths which are determined instead by the natural world.

Whether or not we aspire toward the mastery and leadership this cycle represents, this animal's wisdom, attention to the quest for wisdom, and connection with the spirit of Mother Earth are necessary to the continuing development of our ecospiritual wholeness.

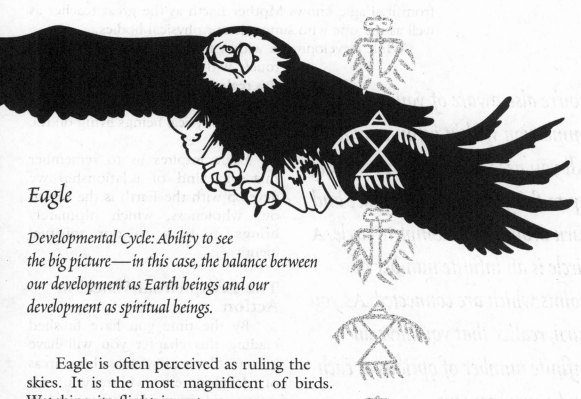

Eagle

*Developmental Cycle: Ability to see
the big picture—in this case, the balance between
our development as Earth beings and our
development as spiritual beings.*

Eagle is often perceived as ruling the
skies. It is the most magnificent of birds.
Watching its flight in nature, we see a creature that has mastered the sky, but has a flaw-
less knowledge of the Earth as well. Without
the knowledge of
how to make
use of the
Earth's gravita-
tional pull, this great bird could not sail or dive. The Eagle
knows equally well the spirit of the sky and the winds and
the solid material spirit of the Earth. It is this balance
between these two forces that gives this bird its formidable
power. We also think of its capacity to see the big picture,
to soar at great heights and survey vast distances.

If we have fully developed the first six developmental
cycles, we know what Eagle knows—that our journey on
Earth is critical to our spiritual development, is inseparable

from it. Eagle knows Mother Earth as the great teacher as well as the one who supports our physical bodies.

While development within the Eagle cycle puts us in touch with the Divine, we soar in this realm only because we have integrated the other developmental cycles as physical beings living on the Earth.

Eagle inspires us to remember that the kind of relationship we develop with the Earth is the key to our wholeness, which ultimately brings us back to our spiritual identity.

You're also aware of your immersion within infinite creation. All you need to do to begin waking up to this fact is stand in place and turn around in a complete circle. A circle is an infinite number of points which are connected. As you turn, realize that you have an infinite number of options at each and every moment.

—Ken Eagle Feather

The Ecospiritual Wheel in Action

By the time you have finished reading this chapter you will have gotten at least a few clues about areas of development where you are strong and those where you want to do further work. You may have even begun to get some ideas about your power animal. Whether you have or haven't begun to get a picture of how this wheel will serve you, the following instructions lay out the entire process. I use this Wheel on a regular basis, by the way, monitoring my own actions and choices every few weeks.

Setting Up the Wheel

Either imagine or create an actual physical circle, and mark the four cardinal points: north, south, east, and west. If you don't know the cardinal points precisely, check it out with a compass, which you can buy at any sporting goods or variety store for less than ten dollars.

As you set up the circle, take time to consider the reasons for setting the area up according to the compass coordinates. This is not a mere formality. On the contrary, by setting the Wheel up in this way, you are creating a specific area in your life where you can reflect on the natural rhythms of the Earth and what they mean in all our lives.

Figure 4.3

Once you have established your north and south positions, take a moment to drop all thoughts about what the compass tells you and even to put aside any preconceptions you might have about medicine wheels or circles. Take some time to position yourself in each of the four directions as you contemplate what they might tell you about the natural rhythms of the planet—your relationship to it and the relationships of the planet with the cosmos. As you do this, you will begin to experience your own dependence on all these rhythms and how you are immersed in the web of life.

Here are some basic rhythms to contemplate: think of

east as the place of the rising Sun, west as the place of the setting Sun, and the north and south as establishing the natural
magnetic pull of the Earth, created because of its relationship
with other celestial bodies. Then consider the center—always
wherever you are standing, since your reference to the world
around you is always from your center. Finally, there are the
regions above and those below, which place you on the surface of the Earth, between the finite rhythm we know as the
tug of gravity and the infinite dimensions of the sky. All life
as we know it takes place within these dimensions.

The wheel you set up can be any size, from a miniature
wheel that you set up on a personal altar in your room, to a
large wheel in a garden area, or a special place on a larger
piece of land. When a wheel is working well for you, you can
picture it in your mind, imagining it in the location of your
choice. Ultimately, this wheel becomes a mental tool that
you hold and make use of within your consciousness.
Wherever you can reference yourself in terms of the above
coordinates, you have all you require to make a medicine
wheel.

Sitting at the Wheel

Now picture yourself taking a seat at the wheel. It may
be at any place on the periphery of the circle. Or you might
even picture yourself above it, looking down from Eagle's
position, or below it, looking up from Mole's position.
Choose whatever position feels comfortable to you. That is
the only criteria for choosing your position at this point.

Once you have taken your position, look around the
wheel and acknowledge each of the positions and each of
the animals sitting with you. Refer to this book to remind
you about the animals and their positions if you wish. After
a few times this part will become automatic.

The Power of Ceremony

I have found that some people like to add their own rituals to this process, such as lighting a candle, smudging, drumming, listening to a tape of nature sounds, offering thanks to each of the animals, or offering a prayer to Mother Earth. Any ritual helps to announce that this is a special time and a process that is different from your everyday life.

While I believe beginning rituals are a matter of personal choice, there is one that is important to do. Remind yourself that there is no hierarchy at the wheel, even though one is implied in the order of the seven positions that we have just discussed. At the wheel, each animal is an equal, no one more important than the other—and that includes you.

Talk to the Animals

Talking to the animals means thinking about each one, reflecting on what they know—suggested in the above sections—and asking yourself how this knowledge is working or not working in your own life. Some people do this internally, simply thinking about it, even referring to the book as they go along. Others carry on imaginary conversations in their minds, going from one animal to another until they feel they have received answers from them all.

In time, if you do this process on a regular basis, the animals will seem to take on lives of their own, but don't worry if this doesn't happen right away. Suggestions for fostering this process are given in subsequent chapters.

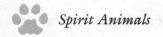

Closing the Circle

After you have completed this process, close the circle by a simple statement of thanks to each of the animals. This can be done in whatever way is comfortable for you, from an imaginary nod of thanks to a prayer of gratitude or a song. Each step along the way should be comfortable and meaningful for you, so do it your way.

Examples of Ecospiritual Wheel Experiences

I don't know about you, but I learn new material best if I can either watch other people who know what they are doing or compare notes with those who have gone through an experience with me. For readers who may wish to compare notes with others, I've provided the following two examples of people's first experiences with the Ecospiritual Wheel.

Dorothy W.

Dorothy is a thirty-two year old fifth grade schoolteacher living in Ohio. Married, she and her husband Jerod consider themselves "environmentally aware." They have a small house on a half acre, about three miles from the school where Dorothy works. Jerod commutes to his city job, fifteen miles away. They have no children, but are planning to start their family in three or four years. The following narrative by Dorothy will give you a fuller picture of her life:

> When I first thought about where I would want to be sitting at the wheel I thought it would be in the eastern part with the Wolf because family is very important to me. I have a very close-knit family, and talk to my two

sisters and my mom and dad almost every week. So, I thought of us all like this pack of really nice wolves.

But I didn't sit there. I found myself wanting to sit between the east and the south, almost next to Badger. That really bothered me at first because Badger seems selfish and tough and I don't think I am either one of these. But that's where I wanted to be, and when I asked myself why, the Badger in me spoke right up. She just told me that I needed to pay attention to my own needs a little more than I do.

[Dorothy stopped at this point and cried a little before going on, commenting, "Well, I didn't expect that!" Meaning the tears.]

Everybody is always telling me I am one of those people who puts everyone else first, and lately I've been just too tired to do it any more. I need a rest, and what Badger is saying to me is that this is important . . . I am important . . . that if I don't take care of my needs . . . well, that this is important . . . [Chokes up.] This is very personal to me. [She tells us she does not want to go into the details because it is so personal.]

I went on and started talking with Mole. I love to garden and I never thought about her the way you talk about in the book. I'm mostly always doing battle with her for burrowing around and getting my plants . . . though I think that might be a gopher. But I started thinking about her in a new way and I feel like she and I are a lot alike. I might even make her my power animal, but I've got to think about that. Sometimes I feel most myself when I am out working in my garden. I really love that!

I thought a lot about Bear and about how it can be good to just retreat from the world . . . go into hibernation . . . to think about things, about balancing your life more. That's about all I did there.

I kept thinking about Wolf the whole time though. Family is so important to me, and I want to have children before Mom and Dad get too old to be able to enjoy them. That's like the continuity that you talk about . . . having them be involved in the next generation. And then it dawned on me that . . . what is the world going to be like for our kids? That's where the continuity and working with Mother Nature really hit home in me!

I went on then to Mountain Lion. I don't know. I think about her in the wild, like you say, and it is difficult to think of myself as a hunter. But I guess there is a part of me that is a spiritual hunter . . . and this is very important to me. It's kind of exciting to think of myself as this wonderful prowling cat looking for answers. [Laughs.]

The Eagle really made me think because it has a lot to do with what I started out with—that I need to pay more attention to my physical needs, just watch that I don't ignore this part of my life . . . that I balance the spiritual and the physical, because I guess if I had a choice I'd just be an eagle or an angel or something and not worry about the physical self. Eagle says that my physical body is part of the spiritual message, and in a way, that's what Badger's message is all about, too. Come to think about it, I see how that ties in with all of this . . . my family and the continuity, all of it. This is very interesting. It all comes back to my relationships with nature and the natural order, doesn't it?

Dorothy finished by saying that she was going to give herself some "homework," to work every day with the Ecospiritual Wheel for a while, to think about what Badger was trying to teach her. She also felt that, while she had always felt that family was the most important aspect of her life, she knew something was out of balance there.

She was extremely concerned about the issue of what she called "continuity." It bothered her to think that her children might be coming into a world where the environment had been, in her words, "spoiled for them." She thought she would join a group to be more proactive in this regard. Finally, she said she was going to look for a good picture of a mountain lion because she wanted to put it in a place where she would see it every day. She liked the idea of thinking of herself as being like a big cat hunting for spiritual answers.

William B.

William is 41, married, with three kids. All the kids are in private school and his wife, Peggy, works part time to pay for their tuitions. William, who is a software engineer, has recently become interested in environmental issues after a favorite recreational area that he had visited since he was a small child was recently closed; the land around it was sold to a housing developer. He chose to stay with a more linear approach, which he titled "Ecospiritual Inventory." The following is his list:

1: Mole. Difficult to even think in these terms, though I get the concept okay.
2: Badger. I remember seeing a movie of a badger going after a rodent of some kind and dirt flying out behind him. Keeping the focus on "number one." I think I do this pretty well.
3: Wolf. Peggy and I have to take a look and figure out ways to spend more time with the kids before they are all too grown up to have anything to do with me. Work, money, all the constant pressure everyone complains about.
4: Bear. Not sure I get this whole thing, except that part of it is about looking at what is going on with our lives, particularly as it pertains to our family.
5: Power Animal. The family dog? [William made jokes about this. He said, "My life being what it is in this

work, I'm mostly one of those guys who shows up to get fed and have his ears scratched, and that's about the extent of it."]

6: Mountain Lion. My hunting skills are pretty damn good, I'd say, meaning earning a good living and protecting my territory. I keep my eye on the cutting edge.

7: Eagle. I think of the "big picture" here. Skills are strong here, work-wise. I have no idea where the big picture is elsewhere in my life. Pretty out of touch, I guess.

It should be noted here that a little over a year after doing this "inventory," as William called it, he joined a group in the Great Lakes area that is dedicated to protecting and restoring wetland areas. Another big change in his life is that he is now writing poetry about his experiences in nature, which he describes as "not for public consumption." (Translation: "No, you can't print it in your book.") He says he is still working on his "ecospiritual material."

Moving Further

Over time, most people develop their own style of working with this Wheel. Don't be afraid to experiment. Whenever the opportunity arises, take time to observe the animals assigned to the wheel in their natural habitat. That doesn't mean that you have to go out and hunt up a mountain lion or a badger, of course, but there are many nature films available that will do the next best thing.

You may have gotten some ideas about your power animal in the process of working with this wheel. In the next chapter we go into this in detail.

5

Personal Power Animals

*Animals live naturally and spontaneously,
doing what they are created to do without the
self-doubt, uncertainty, complaining, and guilt
that characterize human activity. They stand
before us as paragons of creation, living as they
were meant to live . . . never losing their sense of
themselves as spirit, responding with a fullness of
spirit to whatever life presents to them, be it food,
playful fun, sex, or death.*
— Tom Cowan (1996)

One of the world's leading consciousness researchers, Stanislav Grof, M.D., has provided convincing evidence of our capacity to cross boundaries into the consciousness of other humans, as well as that of animals. I became interested in his work because of what it might reveal about shamanism and non-ordinary states of consciousness, and later had the honor of working with him in writing his book, *The Holotropic Mind* (1992).

As a young physician trained in Europe, Dr. Grof seemed destined for a brilliant future in mainstream medicine. Then, in 1956 a package arrived at the prestigious

medical clinic where he was working. It was from the Sandoz Pharmaceutical Laboratories in Basel, Switzerland, and it contained samples of an experimental substance called lysergic acid diethylamide, or LSD-25. The accompanying literature said it had "psychoactive properties" and the makers were interested in finding out if it might be of value in the treatment of some mental illnesses.

Being the youngest and most courageous on the staff, Dr. Grof was elected to be the first guinea pig. What happened then changed his life. Soon after taking the substance, he saw a thunderbolt of light that catapulted him from his body. He then experienced himself merging with the cosmos, racing through black holes and white holes in the Universe, and experiencing the Big Bang. Having lost all awareness of the laboratory and the research assistants where he had begun this strange journey, there was no doubt in Dr. Grof's mind that he was experiencing what great mystical scriptures the world over have called "cosmic consciousness." He would later say of this event:

"Even in the most dramatic and convincing depths of the experience I saw the irony and paradox of the situation. The Divine had manifested itself and had taken over my life in a modern laboratory in the middle of a serious scientific experiment conducted in a Communist country with a substance produced in the test tube of a twentieth-century chemist" (Grof and Bennett 1992).

Dr. Grof's clinical experiences in the subsequent years convinced him that some states of consciousness which modern psychiatry had defined as severe pathology were not that at all. On the contrary, they were glimpses into a world beyond ordinary reality. The visionary worlds of mystics and shamans were, in fact, quite real—just not real the way most of us would think of them.

I remember Dr. Grof paraphrasing William James' comment to describe the dimensions of reality that had opened up to him. He said it was now clear to him that our everyday consciousness is only one specialized type of awareness, while all around us, separated only by the filmiest of screens, there are forms of consciousness that are totally different waiting to be discovered.

What fascinated me most about Dr. Grof's research was our ability to cross consciousness boundaries into the animal world. It was apparently possible to experience the spiritual and archetypal essence of other species. Dr. Grof's observations would provide us in the modern world with a better understanding of the ancient shamanic use of "power animals" as spiritual guides.

In shamanic traditions the world over, people made contact with animal spirits during non-ordinary states of consciousness. Sometimes these states were achieved spontaneously, sometimes through trance-inducing techniques such as drumming or dancing, and more infrequently through the use of psychotropic substances such as psilocybin mushrooms, peyote, and ergot (a fungus growing on rye grain, thought to be used to induce visions in biblical times and before). By entering the consciousness of an animal, and temporarily experiencing the world through its body and mind, the shaman might help locate prey for tribal hunters, diagnose and treat disease, or identify a change that should take place within a tribal community.

Techniques for contacting the spirits of the animals vary from one group of people to another. In societies that use totems and fetishes, it may be done with the help of some object which holds the image of the animal they want to contact. This might be a wood or rock carving or, as in the case of the Lascaux caves, paintings or etchings on the rock walls of caves.

Many of the dances, prayers, chants, and other aspects of ritual life in shamanic cultures revolve around animals—with movements, sounds, masks, and costumes that adopt qualities of the animals' power and wisdom. These are employed in order to communicate with them, or sometimes to re-establish psychic links with them when the connection has been lost through neglect or lack of reverence.

Dr. Grof discovered that such communications with animals were not by any means limited to early cultures. He saw the phenomenon take place in psychedelic sessions, shamanic workshops, in his own holotropic workshops, and in spontaneous psychospiritual crises.[3] He has often witnessed situations in which the power animal experiences were so convincing that they triggered, in previously skeptical Westerners, a deep and genuine interest in shamanism and in the protection of animals in the wild. In a great number of cases, people were so transformed in their beliefs that they went on to pursue further study of this ancient practice with experienced shamans or anthropologists.

All life exists in an intricate system of interdependence, so that the Universe exists in a dynamic state of harmony and balance, reflecting the continuous flow and cycling of energy that emanates from each form of life in relation to every other living being.

—Michael Garrett

Real and Symbolic Encounters with Animals

While Dr. Grof's work validates the shamanic experience, he also points out that there are times when the image of an animal popping into our consciousness is symbolic, that its appearance is expressing something about our own state of being. In dreams, for example, a powerful cat such as a panther might be an expression of intensely aggressive feelings on the part of the dreamer. Or a goat, bull, or stallion might symbolize that person's strong sexual drive or need.

---

[3] Dr. Grof was a leader in getting the American Psychological Association to recognize that spiritual revelations could be real and valid and should not automatically be viewed as pathological manifestations.

While it is not always easy to distinguish between symbolic dream imagery and a transpersonal experience with an animal presence, the best clue that it is symbolic would be if the vision coincides with a strong feeling or challenging experience you've recently had. For example, if a dream of a lion with its teeth and claws bared appears a night or two after you have been in a conflict where you had to hide overwhelming anger you felt, there's a good chance that your dream is symbolic, expressing your previously repressed anger.

People who have a transpersonal experience with an animal spirit generally resist any effort to assign a symbolic meaning to the event. It just is what it is, nothing more and nothing less. Symbolic or psychological interpretations feel like totally irrelevant fabrications when one tries to apply them to these experiences. The person is convinced that they have communicated with the animal on a profoundly deep level and there is nothing to analyze or interpret.

The following is an excerpt from my journal following an experience I had with an animal spirit which was induced through a journeying process that uses visualization and drumming, which I'll describe later in this chapter. The process was further implemented by an animal fetish figure (small stone carving) which I held in my hand:

As instructed by my guide, I held the little stone figure (a mountain lion) in my right hand. The drumming had been going on for about twenty minutes when I felt the first communication. It was powerful and very direct—I would say visceral rather than verbal—as if I could connect with every cell of the animal's body, occasionally becoming that body rather than observing it. In a moment I received a clear mental picture of a beautiful, sleek, very dignified lioness standing almost hidden in a clump of high grasses at the edge of the canyon.

The mountain lion approached me cautiously, pacing back and forth in a relaxed zigzag pattern as she came. Her eyes seemed to regard me lazily, yet I was aware of what I can only describe as an energetic connection between us. If I moved or even had any aggressive thoughts or feelings about her she would sense a shift in this energetic connection and instantly bolt. I was aware of feeling fear and respect for her, but something within me told me I was safe in her presence as long as I maintained my present state of mind, which was simply to learn from her.

When there was no more than a couple yards between us, the animal stopped, looked directly at me and suddenly grew quite tense, with every muscle in her body alert and ready. She stared at me and I remember thinking, "She is targeting my very soul!" For maybe a minute or two I was really frightened, and part of me wanted to stop the session right there. I realized that this creature had the capacity to easily tear me to shreds with her claws and teeth, and I did not know what this might mean from my present state of being if turned against me.

She suddenly thrust her neck forward, bared her teeth and screamed at me, a deafening, blood chilling howl that sent tingling, electric waves up my spine. Then she stopped and I was flooded with feelings of love and appreciation for her, no longer fearful, but in absolute awe of her. Then she lay down, groomed herself briefly, then turned her head and seemed to be gazing past me, as if it was of no concern to her whether I was there or not.

I heard a wonderful rumbling sound from deep in her body and it took me a moment to realize it was purring, as a domestic cat might do except with greater volume—a deep, rumbling tone that resonated in the trunk of my body in an almost sexual way.

While I know this was a journeying vision, it seemed beyond the realm of dream or imagination. The connection I made with the mountain lion opened me up to nature not as a place out in the woods or on the desert or ocean or in the mountains, but as an infinite force within which we all take part. I believe that for me, this event was comparable to what Dr. Grof felt during his first LSD experience, as if

I'd been hit by a thunderbolt that thrust me into the world of the mountain lion.

The line between predator and prey dissolved. Though violence and the fight for survival were as powerful as ever, predator and prey were taking part in a sacred dance that was beyond my comprehension, and possibly beyond human comprehension. I felt that merging with the mountain lion, for even that fleeting time, allowed me to go outside the limits of my own life experience and catch a glimpse of a very different kind of consciousness that was part of the oneness I had first experienced as a child stricken with tularemia.

Biologist Rupert Sheldrake believes that the memories and wisdom of various species are stored in something he calls "morphogenic fields." While these cannot be detected through scientific processes, they are apparently accessible through shamanic techniques. Following the above experience, I say with confidence that I am sure he is right because I felt that I had been given the privilege of getting a peek into these morphogenic fields; and, further, that they are accessible to anyone under certain circumstances.

The experience of this encounter with the mountain lion spirit taught me two things: first, that the boundaries between human and animal consciousness are not as fixed as we might think; second, I felt I better understood what my shaman friend Americo is doing when he starts to move and take on the characteristics of an animal when he is telling stories about them. He is not "acting" them out; he is feeling their presence in his own body. I am convinced that the shaman's intuitive processes of understanding are cellular and spiritual rather than intellectual and rational. The difference between these two ways of knowing is that the latter separates us from the universal order while the former locates us within it.

Personal Power Animals in Your Life

For people from shamanic cultures, personal power animals are the bridge between the universal order, wherein they feel their oneness, and their individuality, wherein they

feel their separateness. The power animal is chosen because it tells something important about the individual person, while one's intimate connection with the consciousness of that animal helps that same person to feel intimately connected with a higher power. To have this soul connection between animal and human is to proclaim a dedication to Earth consciousness, an ongoing relationship that at the very least makes us think twice about any action that might be injurious to this larger order.

Balancing body, mind, spirit, and Earth, as we do in ecospiritual work, is not just the business of ancient man. On the contrary, it may well be more critical than ever in this day of environmental crisis, since it forges our path back to an active, enlivened spiritual relationship with the Earth.

There is a temptation to treat the power animal as if it were a personal charm, or a kind of imaginary pet. While I think there is some value in having these as well, the power animal offers much more—a source of guidance in the creation of a quality of relationship with yourself, others in your life, and our parent planet. And it will become the key position in your use of the medicine wheel. So take care as you make your choice.

In workshops I have seen people choose this animal or that to be their power animal because they liked the looks of the animal or because they had a sentimental attachment that drew them to it. For example, the most popular animals in the Western culture are bears and wolves—choices that are often influenced by the fact that our popular culture is filled with movies, books, and stuffed toys representing these animals. As a result, it's easy to choose an animal because we have been familiarized with it through these channels. However, the commercial presentation of these animals can take us far afield, with false pictures of what an animal is really like. For example, mice in real life are certainly not like Mickey, and bears in the wild are not like Yogi. Anthropomorphizing animals so that they seem more like people than animals defeats the purpose of the power animal, who can reconnect us with a spiritual reality that seems to otherwise elude us humans.

The trouble is that one of these popularized animals might also be a legitimate power animal for you. For example, in many indigenous cultures where people share the environment with bears, these animals quite naturally take on important spiritual dimensions. In fact, the bear is often viewed as a mediator between humans and the higher powers.

How do we determine if our choice in a power animal is right? We do it in a number of ways. If you believe you have a power animal already, ask yourself how it connects with your own life experience. Does it somehow mesh with important events in your inner life? For example, as intense as the mountain lion experience was for me, I have never felt that this was my personal power animal. It does not give me a sense of my center or of what my own life is about. The rabbit, of course, does. It is such an important player in my personal mythology that it could not be denied without denying a key part of my life path.

This brings up an interesting observation. Some people's power animals are anthropomorphized in another way. That is, their animals speak to them as if they were human beings. There are times when this happens with my own power animal, my rabbit. One explanation is that the rabbit is indeed a spirit guide—a shaman who has assumed that form through a process called "shapeshifting." This anthropomorphism of the power animal is common enough that it seems fair to tell you about it ahead of time. Count yourself lucky if it happens, by the way. It's wonderful to have a spirit teacher available to you.

Examples of Power Animals

An architect and builder who attended one of our workshops had grown up in the Upper Peninsula of Michigan where, as a boy, he had been fascinated by the dams built by beavers near his home. He often watched them from a distance through his father's binoculars. He studied the way they wove together the logs and branches and even rocks to make their primitive but elegant structures which were as beautiful to him as any manmade structures he had ever seen. One day he found a dead beaver that had been caught in a trap by a property owner who thought the beavers were causing damage to the forest. The young man was shocked and even grief stricken at the thought that anyone could harm such magnificent and ingenious builders.

Thereafter, he had dreams of beavers and felt that the horror of finding the dead beaver somehow motivated him to become an architect. One of his trademarks is that he works logs into his designs, paying homage to his first teachers, the beavers. Naturally, the beaver prevails as his power animal. It even appears as a logo on his stationary. And although they are becoming increasingly rare even in the wilds of Northern Michigan, he still seeks out the beavers, watching them from a respectful distance whenever he can.

My partner Susan's power animal is a horse. Though she is not a horse woman, nor do we have horses in our life, this animal inspires her in a way that no other does. When she is around them it is fun to watch how she relates to them and them to her. She has no great interest in riding them. Maybe they even sense this, I'm not sure. I've watched them nuzzle her, present their ears for a scratch, or simply stand close enough to barely touch her without pushing. And at times I've seen them show off with a little dance, then turn to her as if to curtsy and let her know that this demonstration was for her benefit. Susan does not talk a lot about what the horse means to her, though she has said that it epitomizes a kind of cooperative relationship between animals and people that also models the sort of relationship she enjoys creating with people and organizations.

A woman I met in New Mexico told me that, even as a small child, she loved to watch deer in the fields near her home. She loved their graceful movements as they ran or leapt over fences. She said that she would watch them whenever she could, but it was not so much the seeing that intrigued her as the fact that she could pretend she was a deer and mirror their movements in her own body. She had dreams of running through forests with herds of deer. Today, she is a dancer and massage therapist, where she says her "deer medicine" constantly inspires her.

To one extent or another, all of these people have learned from the animals, have possibly even communicated with them or imagined themselves inside their consciousnesses. All of these stories are examples of people who connected with their animal spirits serendipitously. But what I have learned both from these people and shamans whom I have known is that we need not depend solely on these serendipitous connections. We can go about it in a more systematic way.

Meeting Your Power Animal

You may already be aware of your power animal. Even if you are not conscious of its identity, look around you for clues. You may have pictures of this animal that you have kept, or even a small statue of it. These can at least point you in the direction of an animal that is particularly meaningful to you.

Family pets are sometimes clues. A dog person, for example, might have a wolf, coyote, fox, or even a dog as a power animal. A cat person might find a mountain lion, bobcat, leopard, lion, cheetah, other member of the cat family, including the cat itself, as a power animal.

I remember as a child collecting small ceramic and cast-metal animals that were popular at the time. I must have had twenty or thirty of them by the time I was eight years old. I only collected wild animals, such as elephants, leopards, rhinos, bison, alligators, lions, wolves, ravens, and monkeys. It was not the figures themselves which interested me, however. Rather, there was something magical that happened when I took one of these figures in my hand and imagined it in the wild. They came alive in my mind's eye,

and I would see them in the wild. Whether in the jungles or swamps or mountains or plains, they always appeared from afar, visions that were elusive and fleeting but powerful influences in a small boy's dreams.

I still recommend the use of animal figures to awaken the image of the animal in your consciousness. I particularly favor figures because they are three-dimensional. When we are working with complex issues, as you may know, our minds work holographically. We construct three-dimensional images (sometimes abstract, sometimes representations) within our consciousnesses. Without going into great detail about this, the hologram gives the image a potential for highly complex associations, and moves us from the restrictions of linear thinking into infinite possibility.

I highly recommend that you familiarize yourself with Zuni fetishes.[4] These tiny stone statues of animals, small enough to fit in your pocket, are carved by the Zuni people in New Mexico and are widely available. However, it certainly does not have to be a stone carving to help you. Anything that evokes the image of your power animal for you can be helpful. Photos, paintings, ceramic or even plastic figures can help.

Set aside some time when you can sit quietly with your animal in a meditative state. If you have a busy schedule, as most people do these days, set aside at least ten minutes a day when you will not be disturbed. No phone calls. Nobody sticking their head in the door to ask where the mustard or the car keys are. No distracting sounds in the background. If you are living in a situation where you do not have that much control of the environment, I suggest wearing earphones and listening to a recording of nature sounds that you might associate with your power animal.

Whenever possible, get out in nature to do this. Find a

---

[4]My book, *Zuni Fetishes: Using Native American Objects for Meditation, Reflection and Insight,* 1996, can be helpful in this.

place where you can sit alone for an hour or more and be with your power animal.

Start out this quest by simply seeking the ways in which this animal is related to your life. For models of how to do this, think of the stories about the woman who always loved to watch the deer or the architect-builder who loved watching beavers, etc. They had very definite connections with these animals, mainly the opportunity to watch them in their natural habitat. You may or may not be so fortunate. Nevertheless, look for the ways that your animal inspires or teaches you.

The best place to find clues for finding your power animal is to think about your own greatest skills and interests, or to look at defining moments in your life that helped you recognize these personal "gifts." I am of the belief that each of us brings a gift into being—something that is hard-wired into our system—that we are intended to give away while we are here on this planet. That gift is our way of expressing our gratitude for our life and the generosity of Mother Earth. The gift can be linked with making a livelihood while we are here, and that is fine since it fits with the lifestyles and economies of the times. But developing the gift, and giving it back in a way that makes a real contribution to the people around us is sacred. That gift, as we have seen in the stories of the people and their spirit animals, may involve virtually any human activity, from healing and massage to building houses or writing books.

If you know what your gift is—and many people don't—seek ways that your power animal epitomizes your gift or in some way allows you to focus your attention on it. For example, think of the way the beaver keeps the architect-builder focused on his gift, or how the imagery of the deer might guide the dancer-massage therapist in the story above.

If you are not clear about what your gift is, ask your power animal to guide you. Do this by getting in touch with the feelings you have about this animal. What are the qualities you most admire in it? What attracts you to it? For example, in a workshop some years ago a woman carved a wonderful figure of an otter. She loved her carving but she could not figure out what it meant to her. Why was it such a powerful influence for her? What had been such a strong attraction that she went to all the trouble of carving it? In a dream she realized what it was. It had to do with the animal's playfulness. The woman herself had a special gift for bringing that sense of playfulness into her work with other people. She was a healer who worked with people in emotional or physical pain and was able to bring this sense of playfulness and joy to them. The playful spirit released her clients from their burdens, sometimes for only a few moments, sometimes permanently. The otter she made not only helped her identify her gift, it helped her focus that gift even more in the years ahead.

The power animal doesn't always focus on lighthearted or positive aspects of your life—at least not initially. Think of the architect-builder as an example. While watching the beavers building their dams certainly inspired him, it was the discovery of the dead beaver that became a prime motivator in his life. Similarly, it is not a rabbit bouncing freely about in the wild that inspired me. Rather, what rises in my awareness is imagery around killing the animal, butchering it, and finally the near-death experience that I had as a result of the illness I contracted from it. These are transformative associations. In other words, it is a gift that arises out of a wound.

Power animals always help put us in touch with the peak experiences of our lives, moments that were filled with joy, with a sense of accomplishment and purpose, or their opposite. Momentous challenges, even grief, bitterness, or horror can be some of our greatest teachers.

Let your dreams and fantasies about your power animal come alive for you. The more alive they become, the more you will find yourself automatically focusing on the power that is around them. The power of your dreams and fantasies will cover a wide range, from your feelings of love for your animal, to feelings of fear and awe. Thoughts of the animal may put you in better touch with your own gifts, acting like a psychic magnet opening your eyes to ways you can develop and express these gifts more fully. Your power animal can fill your dreams (both daytime and sleeping dreams) with a profound sense of the animal's spirit, its particular power in its natural setting.

Understanding Your Power Animal

When you begin working with your power animal you will most likely feel that you are making the whole thing up. That's fine. Don't let this stop you or cause you to doubt what you are doing. It is, in fact, through our imagination that we initiate any new project. Virtually everything we do starts out as an idea or a series of images or feelings in our minds. It then extends, manifesting in action or in expanding the original idea. It is through this same process that we get in touch with a higher level of consciousness.

When C.G. Jung began working with his spirit guide, Philemon, he at first felt that this being was a fantasy—the product of his imagination or a dream figure from his unconscious. But after working with Philemon for a while, he concluded that there were things in our consciousness which we do not produce, but which produce themselves and have their own lives separate from us. At times, he confessed, Philemon seemed real to him, like a living personality, one who accompanied him often in his walks up and down his gardens. This spirit figure, he said, "represented superior insight."

Storytellers throughout history, including modern novelists, often talk about how the characters in their stories take on lives of their own. Things really get interesting at that point. The characters start revealing things about themselves that the storyteller didn't know, sometimes resulting in an author having to totally rewrite the book. During the writing of my novel *Spirit Circle*, for example, the two main characters reversed roles a hundred pages into the writing, forcing me to go back to the beginning and start anew.

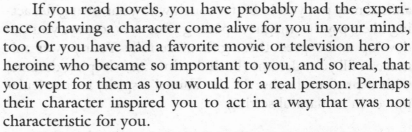

If you read novels, you have probably had the experience of having a character come alive for you in your mind, too. Or you have had a favorite movie or television hero or heroine who became so important to you, and so real, that you wept for them as you would for a real person. Perhaps their character inspired you to act in a way that was not characteristic for you.

Think of your relationship with your power animal as very similar to these kinds of experiences. The more you work with them in that light, the more real and useful they will become for you, providing you with, as Jung said of Philemon, "superior insight."

Some people get nervous about letting their power animals become so important to them. Are power animals infallible? Can their insights always be trusted? The best answer to that is revealed in a little story that Sun Bear used to tell.

It seems that when he was a young man Sun Bear had a spirit teacher who had been a respected elder in his life on Earth. But every time Sun Bear followed his advice, he got into a lot of trouble. So Sun Bear went to his mentor and told him about this. His mentor looked Sun Bear in the eye and, with a bemused grin on his face said, "Well, dead don't make you wise!"

When we have a power animal, it is nice to think that they are a source of superior wisdom, and that their insights are always infallible. But this is not necessarily the way it is. My advice is always that spirit helpers in any form—human or animal—are no more infallible than anyone else in your life. My own power animal, Rabbit, is a trickster, for example. His superior wisdom, and most of his teachings, have to do with the limits of human perception—that this way of knowing , by its nature, is always flawed. He creates illusions and tricks that constantly remind me of this fact, at the very least keeping me humble (most of the time) about what I think I know.

When you think you have identified your power animal,

spend time with it. Sit with the animal in meditation and ask questions such as what it is doing in your life. And listen patiently for answers. If you are a person who likes to write, keep a journal about your work with your power animal.

Understand that your power animal may be very different from other spirit animals that you work with at the Wheel, in that its animal characteristics may be "morphed" together with its human ones. Or they may, as in the examples I've given, focus your attention on your gift. Rabbit's function is always to take me down through his special tunnel that carries me from the seen to the unseen world, just as my bout with tuloremia did when I was a child. Similarly, the architect is inspired in his gift by the beaver, and the dancer and massage therapist is inspired in her gifts by the deer.

What happens if you just don't seem to be able to get a power animal? Patience, of course, is the key. But it may also help to remember that, as children, most of us dreamed about animals, and even may have played that we had become them—a horse, a dog, a cat, or bird. Psychologists say that animals populate the dreams of children until they are about seven years old. After that, they dream mostly of people; parents, siblings, teachers, and if they dream of animals at all after that, it is usually in the context of someone they fear—transforming that person into a fearsome animal.

In your search for a power animal, try going back to those earlier, playful times in your life, when you had an imaginary animal companion. Start with this as your power animal and see where it leads you. In the process, you may rediscover the openness and playfulness that you enjoyed as a child, reopening doors of imagination and spiritual connection that came so naturally to you at that time.

The traditional ways of contacting power animals include drumming, dancing, and vision quests. None of these are mandatory, but if you have an opportunity to join a drumming circle, for example, try it out. Also, you might want to get a drum recording. Using a hand drum or rattle and maintaining a steady beat between 100 and 150 beats per minute will help you maintain a light trance-like state and yet keep you alert.

Dancing, either alone or in a group, with drumming or music, while taking on the movements and persona of an animal is also an effective way to get acquainted with the power animal.

And finally, the vision quest, particularly to a wilderness area that is particularly meaningful for you, gives you and your power animal a chance to get acquainted. Vision quests consist of going out into the wilderness and spending at least one night alone. Traditional vision quests usually included fasting, ceremony, prayers, and subjecting oneself to considerable hardship in the loneliness of the wilderness. If you are seriously considering a vision quest, I recommend doing your first ones with a leader. There are an increasing number of people offering vision quests as workshops, and with a little detective work on your part you should be able to find such resources near you.

Should you wish to do it on your own, be sure to take the usual precautions of letting others know where you are going and how long you expect to be gone. For an initial vision quest, take along sufficient water, a sleeping bag, and basic needs for a single day and night. Make yourself a comfortable, but minimal campsite and set up a medicine wheel (as described in the previous chapter). Start your work with the Ecospiritual Wheel, also described in chapter four. Minimize all other activities, concentrating on your work with the wheel, meditating, and keeping your mind and your heart open to invite in your animal spirit.

Synchronicity—the apparent acausal relationship of events—can play a part in the search for a power animal. For example, a friend of mine, Joyce, has a hummingbird as a power animal. This animal began appearing to her whenever she was facing a particular challenge in her life. Since she formally adopted it as her power animal she turns to it regularly for help and guidance. Oddly enough, it has made its appearance in some of the most unlikely places, such as outside the window of an office building, three stories above the street when she was being interviewed for a job in Silicon Valley. What this animal was doing three stories up, in a place where there were certainly no flowers to be found, remains a mystery to this day. But its appearance did help Joyce to remember her own power and land the job she wanted.

As you begin working with your power animal, be sure to integrate it into your work with the Ecospiritual Wheel. Your power animal will have much to teach you about your own voice and how you can more fully realize the wholeness that is your potential in each of the developmental cycles at the wheel. Speak with your power animal, either silently or aloud, or perhaps by writing in your journal.

In time, your work with your power animal and the wheels of life that I describe in this book will become second nature. You'll find yourself tailoring these practices to your own way of doing things, and I encourage this. From what I have seen, the more people develop their own wheels and their own way of working, instead of simply following someone else's system, the more they are empowered in their lives. Though I think teachers, such as myself, can give people a place to start, the most important lesson of all may be to respect your own creativity and intuition. Each of us has a unique gift to bring to this world through our own voice and we cannot do that except by honoring ourselves.

6

Prophecy and Divination at the Edge

> *We are embedded in nature, and again so solidly that the line between the two is not easy to establish, indeed . . . does not exist.*
>
> **—Huston Smith (1991)**

Susan and I live in a small town in Northern California, a little over two hours from the Golden Gate Bridge. Our little house sits at the edge of an oak forest, a short distance from a large wilderness area. Every spring, a woman across the canyon from us plants flowers which she sells at the farmers' markets. At six-thirty every morning, after the first blooming of the season, she goes out and beats on a tin kettle to chase away the wild turkeys, which love to eat the colorful flowers. The woman says her dog used to keep the big birds away, but he has grown old and after spending half his life chasing the turkeys off, only to have them return, he has decided there are better ways to spend his time. As the woman beats on her pan, the turkeys, as many as forty of them, take flight and move down into the underbrush to wait for the noise to stop. Laying comfortably on the redwood deck, the old dog raises his head to watch their flight.

Like the woman across the canyon, Susan plants flowers, too. She does not mind if the turkeys take a few, but last summer when they dug up the early bulbs she had planted, she tied string between the trees and hung strips of shiny mylar to make it clear to the birds that this was her territory and they were to honor it. She goes out and talks to the turkeys, pointing out that there is plenty for them to eat on the hillside below her gardens. I can't be sure, but the turkeys seem to respond to her approach better than to the woman who bangs on pans. The flock walks through our property to forage on the hill below our compost pile but they mostly leave Susan's flower beds alone.

We don't really want the turkeys to leave. Mid-summer, when the chicks have hatched and grown big enough to forage with their parents, the hens herd them around with gentle chirpings that are very pleasant to hear. And the big toms spread their tail feathers and strut about, displaying their manhood.

In addition to flowers, Susan grows garlic and basil and tomatoes and potatoes and squash. We had to put up seven-foot wire fencing around that garden to keep out the deer. The deer seem to understand our fences and don't challenge them. Susan hasn't had to talk with them. But the neighbors just to the north of us have a large pasture which may account for them not bothering our gardens. There are up to a half-dozen deer on the hillside sometimes. I think they prefer the open pasture to our cultivated yards.

There are occasionally small battles in our neighborhood between the serious cultivators and the animals. The deer seem to wait each year for one of our neighbors who plants nice neat rows of pansies along the garden rows close to her house. As soon as the flowers are in the ground the deer appear on the manicured lawn, standing very still and looking like garden statuary as cars pass, then going back to nibbling on the sweet pansies before moving down into the pasture again.

It is not just us humans who have skirmishes with the

wildlife. The domestic animals have their challenges as well. Every morning, our neighbors on the road across from us leave food on their front porch for their cat. After they leave for work, a large raven, who has been awaiting their departure, glides down from the trees. The cat stands back and watches while the big black bird scolds in its rasping voice, swaggering as it feasts on feline kibble.

Another neighbor used to have trouble with a family of raccoons that raided her cats' dishes. She made her peace with them by putting out enough food for both the cats and the 'coons. That was years ago. The animals have apparently worked it out, since both the cats and their masked cousins are healthy and apparently happy with the arrangement.

From our kitchen window each morning I look across the distance to Snow Mountain thirty-five miles away. It's a wilder place than this. There is usually snow at the top of Snow Mountain from December through April or May. The animals rarely encounter humans out there except during hunting season. Neither do they enjoy the benefits, such as cat kibble or the honey-sweet blooms of pansies.

There's a marsh down below us and in the summer we are serenaded by at least a million frogs and crickets. Evenings, they sometimes sing so loud they blot out conversation. Well, nearly! I find their music soothing. When our young grandson came to visit last summer, he told us the noise was "annoying." They don't have sounds like that in the suburbs of Portland where he lives.

We have worked out an uneasy truce between the cultivators (us humans) and our wilder brothers and sisters, the turkeys and deer and ravens and crows and raccoons and rabbits. And yes, with the frogs and crickets, too. For the most part, I think we are all happy with the arrangements. But I worry. The vineyards have been expanding, buying up every square foot of land they can find to put in their increasingly valuable crops. I'm afraid for the animals, that their rights to this place will not be respected. There's a kind of balance for the time being, but I'm afraid it won't hold. If I see that the animals are having to move further north I think I'll follow them.

The Wheel at the Edge

In so many ways, my home is the perfect setting for the kind of work we have been exploring in the book. The fragile peace here, between the world of the animals and the human world, is a microcosm of the global picture. The ecospiritual issues that exist in this place, and which are mirrored in millions of places similar to this, should be pressing us to open our eyes—not only to the slow disappearance of the animals but to the shrinking of our planet's diversity. As this diversity shrinks, so do our chances of finding answers to our present problems. And unless we act to protect them, we will most certainly lose those still-wild spirits of the animals who can guide us back to our center.

Living close to the edge as we do, one begins to see what is happening from the perspective of the animals. From the human perspective, we sit at the edge of civilization. From the animal's perspective, their wilderness home is shrinking. At the precarious edge between civilization and wilderness, the animals are seeking us out. They appear in our dreams, explore our gardens, and visit our back porches where we feed our pets. Last summer, this was driven home in the most dramatic and poignant way possible, convincing me, once and for all, that the animals are as interested in us as we are in them. But before I go on, let me set the scene. Soon after we moved here, four and a half years ago, I built a medicine wheel a hundred yards or so from our house, halfway down the canyon. The wheel itself is a clearing in the woods about thirty feet in diameter. There's a circle of rocks with each of the four directions—north, south, east, and west—marked with larger stones. There are also several stumps cut from an oak tree that fell last year. They serve as places to sit for people who might like to join me.

This is a sacred place to me, made so by its use. I pray here. I come here to meditate. I bring the spirits of the animals to this place and seek their counsel. I find my soul here when in the midst of my frequently too-busy life I get lost. And whenever I am away from it, say in another part of the country, this spot is my reference point. I need only to align myself with the four points of the compass wherever I am, and I can feel almost like I am back at this place. Once established, a sacred place is held in the consciousness, becoming part of our inner landscape.

East and West

When I first started learning about the medicine wheel, my mentor told me to start by carefully observing nature. For the wheel to serve me, it should be grounded in the rhythms of nature. He told me to watch the movements of the sun. Each morning it rises in the east, announcing a new beginning. In the evening, of course, it moves off to the west, bringing closure to that day. Thus, at the most basic level, the east becomes the place of new beginnings, the west the place of closure. From the center of the wheel, these truths become more than facts: they are constant reminders that beginnings and endings, openings and closings, births and deaths, are all cycles in the natural order. But even these are only rhythms within a larger order that is an endless circle, like the wheel itself, with no beginning or end.

North and South

North and South tell us of the yearly cycles of the seasons. In the summer months, the sun is highest over our heads, providing us with the longest days and the greatest heat. In the winter months, the axis of the Earth shifts. Our sun moves south across the Northern Hemisphere's horizon, and we find it low in the southern sky, rising later, and setting sooner than in the summer months. During the winters, the shadows are long around the wheel. Shivering and damp, we sit at the wheel, and are reminded that the sun is the source of all energy on the planet, including the energy that animates our own bodies. South is the place of heat and the place of the life force itself.

In the winter months, the North is the place of cold and rain and snow. But the snow and rain are important, too. Water and fire join with the mysterious alchemy of the Earth to produce all that nurtures and sustains us. It is from the rhythms of the sun, in both directions across the sky—East to West in the diurnal cycle, North to South in the annual cycle—that we keep balance in our lives, reminding us to honor our place within the cosmos. Orienting ourselves with these daily and seasonal cycles is important because it is here that we are reminded of our dependence on a higher order outside ourselves. These cycles remind us that our own lives are bound to these rhythms by the invisible Creative Source that orders the Universe.

Contemplating the Circle

Sitting at the wheel each day, be it in our minds or on the land, we cannot miss the planetary cycles and rhythms of life. We become aware of how our planet is woven into the web of life, one great body moving through space, responding to ever-changing forces that extend far beyond known boundaries. The wheel connects us with the Mystery and humbles even our grandest achievements. Sitting at the wheel, allowing

It seems that the more a Spirit-related agenda manifests in mainstream endeavors, the more people are able to gain control of their lives. Yet often we want to impose the conditions of our success on Spirit, rather than let Spirit continue delivering our education. We focus on how we want things to be, rather than giving ourselves to Spirit in order to find out how to be.

—*Ken Eagle Feather*

ourselves to contemplate these truths, it is difficult to think of ourselves (we humans) as superior to anything. Certainly we are not greater than the web of life, of which we are such an insignificant part. We are born out of the stuff of this world—every molecule that makes up our bodies a part of it; subject to its laws, and so, somehow, included in the total plan.

The lessons of the medicine wheel are not superstitions or romanticized throwbacks to paleolithic times. Rather, they are ways to remind us of the natural rhythms that govern nature and therefore all our lives. As a spiritual practice, the wheel that is created from personal observations of the natural world not only broadens our awareness of our interdependence but guides us closer to the experience of our oneness, and thus to our bond with all living things and our Earthly home.

Above and Below

Besides the four primary points, there is also above and below. These remind us that we are living in a holographic universe, not a two dimensional one. Each part is a microcosm, mirroring the whole, perhaps even containing all the secrets of the whole, the code of Creation itself, as was Einstein's contention. These codes for the whole are contained even in each of the smallest units that make up our own bodies. Each one projects its content outward to create and maintain the universe we see. The seeds of vast, limitless Creation are held by every cell in each of our bodies, as well as by every other unity of energy or mass, infinitely large or infinitely small.

To look above reminds me that we are living in a world with no beginning, middle, or end, where, as the physicists tell us, particles (mass) and waves (energy) are the same, shifting from one to another freely, depending on how we choose to perceive them. View them as particles and they take the form of particles. View them as waves and they take the form of waves. This is especially clear to me when I sit at the wheel at night and gaze upward into limitless space, at the same time feeling myself pulled toward the center of the Earth. I am humbled and excited at such moments, realizing that beyond what our minds and our senses can perceive is an invisible reality that would forever elude us, except for the fact that we know all this could not exist if such an unseen reality were not there. I am humbled because, in my humanness, I realize I can never fathom the full dimensions of Creation. Yet I am excited by the mystery.

And now I shift my attention from the regions above to the regions below. Below us is the Earth herself. I like the term "Mother Earth" because it seems to me this explains our true relationship to her. She literally supports and nurtures us. Only she knows the alchemical secrets of the nutrients and healing substances that come from her body and are given to us through plants, minerals, waters, gases, and animals.

Once you realize that you are part of everything and everyone, the dynamics between you and every other person change. You realize that how you treat another is a reflection of how you treat yourself. All things become extensions of your own intelligence. You realize we are all part of the quantum field of reality in which each person functions as a major determinant of that reality.

—V. Vernon Woolf

Center

Finally, there is the center of the wheel. This is a key position. To have a sense of direction, to even be able to distinguish between north, south, east, west, above, and below, we need this position—which is always wherever we are standing at any given moment. It is the place where you make the first and last and every step of your journey.

Unlike the other stations on the wheel, it is constantly shifting because something about us is always changing, and will be doing so for as long as we walk the Earth. These changes may involve the focus of our attention—which might shift momentarily as a bird flies overhead, or as we remember something we need to do that day, or as a dark memory passes over us, suggested by something that has been said in the circle.

Changes may also include physiological processes, such as a change in our body chemistry as we become more relaxed, or ongoing digestive processes which continue as we sit at the circle. And finally, as new information or revelations emerge from the circle, we may literally change our minds and thus our perceptions about something in our lives, thus transforming us spiritually.

The center is a constant reminder that, as humans, our understanding of the world, even our sensory perceptions of it (how it looks, smells, tastes, sounds, feels), are always filtered through the lens of our own life experiences. Because of this and because of our changing nature, we can never do more than catch fleeting glimpses of the larger Truth: the Truth that some call God, the unseen or the invisible reality or the power greater than ourselves.

Accepting the incomplete or flawed nature of our personal centers, we come to the Wheel of Life hunting for a bigger picture. When several souls come as equals to this circle we may learn three things: first, humility about our own limits, second, compassion for the limits of others, and

third, that our collective vision offers each of us a tool for seeing beyond our own singular limitations.

If you remember that your spiritual being is the center, all the other positions of the circle are always with you, just as the compass points, the sky above and the Earth beneath you are always present. (For further discussion, see chapter 7: The Metaphysics of the Wheel of Life.)

Choosing A Place at the Wheel

When I'm at my wheel at home, I often sit nearest the southern quadrant, facing north. Notice that I do not sit at the center. The moment we take a place at the circumference of the circle, we each acknowledge that we hold an equal position at the wheel. Each of us also forms a radial, that is, a line or ray of energy extending to the center of the wheel; we each bring who we are.

It is best to follow your intuition when choosing where to sit at the wheel. Whenever I take a position there, I seek an explanation of what I can give or receive from that place. Sitting in the South, for example, I face the North, the place of the quest and the place of wisdom as I see it. My perception of this is that I am identifying with the concept of the hunt, and that what I am seeking is a truth greater than my own limited perceptions. There can be other explanations, of course, but for now this is what I choose to accept as the reason for sitting where I do.

To my right is the east, the place of new beginnings. This feels right to me, for a rather prosaic reason—that I am right handed and being a writer what I create (new beginnings) comes from the right side of my body. I also perceive myself turning to the left for closure and completion in my life. Why that is so I cannot say, but I know that it is true about myself.

To sit near the southern quadrant accomplishes two things for me: it places the sun at my back, warming me, but also allows me to keep my eyes open (not looking into the glare of the sun), and it places me in a position of healing and change.

As I take my place at my wheel at home, I look around me at the natural landscape. This is an important part of the ritual—to acknowledge one's relationship to the physical world. Up on a hillside maybe half a mile away there's an old fir tree. It's directly north, and so when I first sit down at the wheel I glance up and greet it, realizing it has been standing there longer than I have been on this planet. In this landscape, the tree is an elder that elicits my respect.

All around me are forests of oak and manzanita, along with grasses and brush of various species, this great variety of plant life all supported by Mother Earth. Off to my right, across the canyon, I can see paths through the gardens of the woman who raises flowers to sell at the farmers' markets. To my left are Susan's gardens, the flower gardens directly left, the vegetable gardens northwest. The message that I seem to consistently derive from this is that I have come from the cultivated place, where we impose our own sense of order, to a wilder place with an order that exceeds my understanding.

The seven spirit animals that come to sit with me at the wheel are the same ones I described in chapters 4 and 5. As I sit at the wheel, I begin with a greeting for each of the animals, thanking them for being in my life. I can picture each one clearly in my mind's eye, and even feel their presence. The more you work with your spirit animals the more real they become, until they literally take on lives of their own and wander about freely in the wilder parts of your inner world.

I like to smudge[5] the area before beginning to work with the animals. Smudging consists of burning sage and other aromatic herbs and grasses to spiritually cleanse the area. There is a clay pot that I keep at the southern quad-

---

[5]Smudging: You will find a longer explanation about smudging, and how I use it, in appendix A.

rant where I sit. I also have a large flat stone there, where I can cut some dry sage, light it and put it in the smudge pot. When it is smoking nicely, I walk around the circle clockwise, stand in each station for a moment, and smudge that area, imagining that the spirit animal is there.

Many native Americans smudge for spiritual cleansing, bringing new air to the place, signaling the spirits of our presence, and inviting them to join us. I also feel that the ritual of smudging is important because it announces that we are entering a sacred space. This message is important for you as well as those beings who are a part of your inner reality.

I smudge all the way around the circle, the middle of the circle, then raise the smudge pot to the sky. Lastly, I make a special offering to Mother Earth of some freshly crumbled sage and organic tobacco, sprinkling it near the center of the wheel.

Now I sit down, relaxing and meditating, emptying my mind as much as I am able to do. Slowly, the circle comes alive within my consciousness. The spirits of the animals become almost palpable to me, like presences which I cannot see with my eyes or touch with my hands, but which I know are there. The feeling is like being in a house and knowing there are other people in other rooms, even though you can't see them or hear them.

I try to come to the circle without specific questions, such as, "Should I take the job in New York that has been offered me?" Or, "What should I do about my best friend who is angry at me?" I have learned that in most cases, the problem or conflict I am experiencing is at least partly the result of how I am shaping the question in my own mind. This is one of the things we learn from Mountain Lion, who "tracks" its quarry, that is, we hold an issue (our quarry) in our mind but we know that forming specific questions about it would be making certain presumptions about it, presumptions which very possibly blind us to the very answers we seek.

At the wheel, I start my quest simply by describing what is going on with me and then asking the others at the wheel to reflect on what my situation brings up for them. There are no "answers" at the wheel, no advice-givers here, nor are there any resolutions. We don't come away with decisions or choices having been made. We come away with one thing: a larger vision, a larger perspective about our own life. Resolutions follow in time, and according to a different plan than you may have had in mind, but they do come.

The process might be described as something along the lines of one thing leading to another. We learn this process from Mountain Lion. She picks up a scent, follows it, comes to a spot where the animal she is tracking stopped to urinate, leaving a stronger scent. One track carries the hunter to another track and another and another until she sees a movement in the bushes ahead and knows she has found her prey. "One thing leads to another" is very much in alignment with the natural rhythms, not only of Mountain Lion, but for the Universe itself.

It took me a while to get used to this method of working. Each time I come to the circle now, I remind myself that all I need to do is bring who I am, my physical, emotional, and spiritual presence to the wheel, and in a short time I will pick up the trail.

It has also become clear to me over the years that the spirit animals do not necessarily view themselves as my personal guides or helpers. Any help I receive might just as well come by observing them and by being in their presence— seeing the world through their eyes, with or without their awareness of me. Over the years I have had a few human friends like this, people I might visit when I am feeling upset or blue. While we don't directly discuss the issues, I always go away feeling better, and as often as not, I begin to see my problem in a new light that reveals a solution.

For me, one of the important disciplines I've had to learn at the wheel is to trust what at first appeared to be an impossibly indirect way of approaching problems. Over time it has taught me patience, the need to respect the rhythms of a higher order, and that the consciousness of the animals can be a guiding force to the unseen reality.

Sometimes I come to the wheel simply to be there, to be reminded of the lessons I have learned at this place. When I do come asking for help, I describe my problem in the form of "I" statements. What that means is that I express what I feel about the problem, keeping the focus on my own emotions. For example: "I am feeling afraid that I won't be able to complete the job on schedule." Or, "I am angry with my business associate for not meeting the deadline we agreed to." Sometimes I state these things aloud. Sometimes I state them only in my mind.

Listening

One of the most challenging parts of learning to work with the spirit animals was developing my inner receiving and hearing capacities. I found myself, at first, wanting to put words into the mouths of the animals, projecting onto them my ideas of what they are about, instead of waiting for them to tell me. To some extent, that is still a problem. But is it a problem? If we deny that it is happening, we rob ourselves of the possibility of looking at our projections and of taking responsibility for them. For instance, as we set out to create a medicine wheel, or even to adopt a traditional wheel from a culture that we have been raised in, we make choices. I choose the animals I wish to sit at the wheel. It would be foolish to claim that we don't choose our teachers. We do.

Certainly, the issues we struggle with in our lives will result in our seeking or attracting certain teachers (or avoiding them, if we are fearful of change). The spirit animals have convinced me that Jung's discoveries about spirit guides are correct—that such guides may produce themselves and have their own lives, separate from us. Like Jung, I am convinced that they can represent superior insight not

derived from any other form of information gathering, such as books, television, talking with other people, going to school, etc.

Each spirit animal embodies instincts and qualities that are part of Creation's total expression. In many cases, the animals capture the essence of one or two key aspects of Creation and by being in these animals' presence, they may open our hearts and minds to those instincts or qualities in ourselves. We then discover a common bond between us—not only that we share these instincts, but that together we mirror a greater consciousness.

In the Zuni culture, and others whose spiritual disciplines are based on their relationships with animals, it is believed that the animals are closer to the Creator than humans are. They are direct expressions of this greater consciousness, and do not carry on complex inner debates with themselves about whether or not to follow that guidance. Meanwhile, the Zunis speak of human beings as being more "finished" than the animals. We have the capacity to make choices and decisions without guidance from the greater consciousness from which the animals take their guidance. We have only to look around us, at the mess we have made of the Earth, for examples of how our capacity to make choices without reference to the higher order can affect us. Acting only for our own personal gain, we have damaged or destroyed vital natural resources.

In the Earth-based spiritual traditions, we look for the clues that may tell us when we are on a path that is in harmony with the higher order and when we are off. By following these traditions, we are no longer guided only by our own self-interests.

And so I sit with the animals at the wheel. I try to imagine them in their natural habitats. If I have experienced them in nature, I may draw from the memories of what I saw. After a few moments, I feel myself slip out of the pace and rhythm of my everyday world and drop into a rhythm that is very different. I feel this throughout my body, at a deep, cellular level. My mind slows and an incomparable contentment comes over me. Immersed in these rhythms, I may find myself turning my attention to one animal or the other, or sometimes more than one at a time.

Working the Wheel

We have all had a family member or a friend going through difficult times. Questions arise about how much advice or other help to give. How much should I say when I believe they are making a wrong choice? How much should I encourage them to pursue a new path? Should I risk getting into the middle of a conflict that is really theirs to resolve on their own without my advice or help? Are they calling me just to have me listen while they talk out something that is troubling them?

These are all questions that are commonly encountered in friendships and family life, and while our responses to them are usually more reflexive than reasoned, there are certainly those times when a more thoughtful approach is prudent. The following is an example of how you might use the medicine wheel to help you out.

Confronted by a loved one seeking my help, it would be very natural for me to first turn to Wolf. I believe that in the wild he represents the healthier instincts of family and community life. I imagine him in his own habitat. Everything he does follows an instinctive drive to honor the continuation of his own species. This concern extends quite beyond supplying the basic needs such as food, shelter, and protection from one's enemies. It also involves passing along skills of individual strength that serve this continuum, such as hunting cooperatively as a pack. Wolf's instincts are for teaching, nurturing, encouraging—nearly always aimed at passing along skills which serve the continuum rather than serving exclusively selfish pursuits. For example, you would not expect to find a wolf teaching one of its young how to take advantage of other members of the pack, amassing a fortune for its own aggrandizement. Rather, he teaches individual behavior which contributes to the strength and health of the whole pack.

Working with Wolf I become aware of how important it is to think in terms of a continuum. Wolf's principles, as it were, protect, nurture, and teach skills that serve the future as well as they serve the present. Sitting at the wheel with him, I am reminded to keep my advice to my friends and family members focused for the greatest good.

I turn then to Bear, this creature who lives a rather solitary life, seemingly dedicated only to her own well-being and the well-being of her cubs. While there are times when she may seek community, it is not an everyday part of her life. She stands in her own power, representing what seems to me an instinct that tells us something about the importance of our own well-being. We honor our separateness in a special way, careful not to sacrifice it needlessly. Sitting at the wheel with Bear, I am reminded to counsel my loved ones about the importance of standing in their own power. I would urge them to pursue their true voice, their unique gift, rather than reacting blindly to their fears, resentments, jealousies, or temptations of short-term gratification.

Bear's presence at my wheel acts almost like a magnet that pulls in and alerts me to make distinctions between the two kinds of power: self-power and power over others. Power over others breeds conflict, war, and exploitation. It is power of the ego and it comes from attempting to dominate others, including nature. By contrast, self-power breeds fulfillment through our God-given gifts. For the rewards of the latter we need only remember the ecstatic heights we experience listening to truly accomplished musicians, or the joy we experience in our own achievements which truly come from our hearts.

Badger, clawing furiously around the roots of a fallen tree in search of its supper, is not my favorite animal. But, as I turn my attention in his direction, I am reminded that we each have a drive within us that is just as tenacious as this animal's. It comes with taking the form of an individual living on this planet. It is a manifestation of the life force itself, an expression of the greater consciousness which we hold in sacred trust.

Badger teaches me to pay attention to the preciousness of the life force, in all its various manifestations. It reminds me to view life as sacred even when I might view certain forms as threatening (a poisonous snake) or at least annoying (a mosquito). One of the great contradictions of life on Earth is that we must sacrifice life in order to live. Whether it is an animal or a vegetable being sacrificed for our evening meal, this cycle of exchange is sacred, not to be taken lightly, whether it involves a cabbage or a lamb.

The great religions all try to teach us to honor the Creative Source—call it God, Allah, the Great Spirit—above all else, even as you respect life in its individual forms. It is not an easy concept for us humans to grasp, since it requires us to juggle contradictions. The wheel of life itself may be the best way to do this: It teaches us how to look at our own limitations while it offers us guidance to move forward, honoring a power greater than our own selfish needs and desires.

When counseling a loved one, Badger's presence reminds me that our most primal impulse favors our own preservation above all others. Whenever a person feels they are in trouble of any kind, this impulse comes to the fore. To be truly helpful, it's necessary to acknowledge this part of our makeup and move on from there.

Mole reminds me of how dependent we all are on the alchemy of the Earth. Her "grounding" is much more than being centered and content in her our own body and mind. It is also an awareness that to live in balance is to remember where we receive the support of our physical bodies—from the Earth's bounty—and to injure the Earth is to threaten our very existence.

I do not always know quite how to apply Mole's teachings when counseling a loved one. I do believe, however, that every one of us, at least at some deep instinctual level, is aware of how we have abused Mother Earth. We are aware that we have injured the source of our well-being, and this cannot help but cause a kind of floating anxiety that we often can't even name. Maybe it's enough to recognize that this is an issue that adds to the burden of whatever other anxieties our loved ones are feeling. And maybe it is through writing or reading books like this one that we attempt to find solutions to this problem.

Eagle reminds me that, if we are to develop spiritually, we must learn that our present task is to live in our bodies on the Earth. In this age, so much of our energy goes into learning to live on the Earth, particularly in modern life where technology has become a dominant force, with challenges that take us far beyond the more universal rhythms of life.

When counseling a loved one, I like to keep in mind that the technological world embodies values which we humans have created on our own, generally without reference to the higher order. As such, the ethics it fosters fly in the face of all reason and spiritual wisdom. We spray the countryside with chemicals that we have created in the laboratory in order to make farming more productive and profitable, ignoring the fact that it threatens the fragile alchemy of the soil and water and air. We inject animals with hormones and antibiotics, ignoring long term effects on humans. It becomes all too easy to believe that all this is the "real world," and that it somehow offers the fulfillment we all seek. So, I am reminded by Eagle that there is more, and that even with those loved ones who are not on spiritual paths I can insist that there is more to life than owning the latest gimcrack from Silicon Valley.

Mountain Lion reminds me that the hunt, the quest, is a daily activity, not something you do once for all times. While counseling loved ones I have a tendency to lose sight of the fact that each person is on his or her own quest, one that requires them to do their own tracking and pay attention in their own way. This is something I should know very well since I was raised in a family of woodworkers, people who understand that to produce a beautiful finished product you need to pay attention to every step along the way. That's Mountain Lion's lesson, too; that we will only catch our quarry if we pay attention to every scent on the trail.

To counsel a loved one about something that is not yet on their trail is not only distracting, it dishonors their process. Mountain Lion advises us to pay careful attention to whatever scent or track our loved one is following. How easy it is to presume that we know how others should live their lives! We serve best when, like Mountain Lion, we teach how to hunt rather than just putting meat on the table.

And lest I forget, Mountain Lion also reminds me to patrol my boundaries and to respect the boundaries of others.

Finally, at the center, my power animal, Rabbit, sits observing me with more than a hint of irony. What little tricks of the mind will he play that challenge me to question whatever wisdom I might glean from this process? Rabbit reminds me of the limits of my own perceptions—regardless of their original source.

Here, at the center, the power animal also reminds me that we must each seek our own voice, our own gift. Even with all the help from the others around the wheel, our own lives, and thus our greatest strength, are incomplete without our own voice. And so, in counseling loved ones this is a very high priority for me. I cannot help but ask, "Is what I am telling this person helping them to find their own voice? Does what I am telling them honor my own?"

So what do I come away with? What does my work at the wheel tell me about counseling loved ones? First and foremost, giving advice is not to be taken lightly. Listen carefully. Honor the individual struggle that is every human's lot, but watch out for things which may look like solutions but which fail to honor Mother Earth, the life force itself, and the balance between spiritual development and the business of being an Earth creature. Keep boundaries defined. Hold the continuum sacred, that is, honor what Creation has given us here on Earth and do your best to do nothing that injures it.

All of this is a tall order, and converting it into the answers that my loved ones can make use of isn't always easy. Sometimes, simply standing in my power at the center of my wheel is the best I can do. I say little but listen carefully, acknowledging their struggles, their strengths, and their weaknesses. And often, the best I can offer is to remember my intent, my strengths, and my shortcomings, so that I don't interrupt the present rhythms of their lives.

A Prophecy and Lessons from Life

On or about the day that I started planning this book, early in the summer, I encountered a young doe as I made my way along the path to my wheel. She stood not fifty feet away, watching me, but did not startle or move away. Her belly was large and I wondered if she was pregnant or just overfed. She stood her ground even as I sat down at the circle and began the rituals of the wheel.

The one who fears no truth fears no lies.

—American Folk Saying

I forgot all about the young doe. An hour or more passed as I consulted with the other animals about a matter which had been troubling me. I was vaguely aware of the deer moving clockwise around the circle, then disappearing into the thick brush behind me. Later, when I got up to leave, I turned slightly and saw that she was laying in the tall grass behind me, not a dozen feet away. She watched me as I walked back up the path to the house.

I saw the doe occasionally after that, but never that close again. Several weeks passed. Then one day as I sat at my wheel, she walked past me with two beautiful, healthy looking fawns. She stopped, turned her head in my direction, as if to make certain I saw and acknowledged her young family. I smiled, touched by her apparent trust of me.

Then she moved toward the pasture, careful not to move more quickly than was comfortable for her still wobbly-legged twins.

Her appearance affirmed so much of what the animals had been teaching these past fifteen years at the wheel, that regardless of our species there are bonds we all share. The pride and delight she took in her parenthood crossed the boundaries between our species, for I, too, was touched to see her youngsters and took pleasure in her delight. Judging by the number of times she appeared that summer, parading her little troupe past me, she may have sensed my enjoyment.

The thicket near the wheel appeared to be her home base. Her and the twins' footprints along the trail through the woods indicated that we shared the same path. And as if the footprints were not proof enough of her presence, I discovered one afternoon that she had left a little—shall we say, "gift?"—in my smudge pot. This was no mean feat since its opening was less than four inches across.

As Autumn approached I found more animals—the *real* ones, in physical bodies—participating at the wheel. A large raven appeared several times, coming as if summoned by the scent of my smudging. Within minutes of lighting the sage, I would see her flying in from the Cow Mountain wilderness area northeast of us. Each time she came, she perched in a tall oak tree, watching me at the circle. When I was finished, she would signal her departure with a few loud caws and leave. She could have been the same one who stole the neighbor's cat food, I'm not sure, but it is clear that she was also drawn by something about my activities.

As winter approached, Susan and I discovered that an important business associate of ours was operating in a way that was less than ethical, and possibly even criminal. As we investigated further, we found that we were probably going to lose several thousand dollars. The specter of dealing with attorneys loomed on the horizon as we made one effort after another to resolve the problems in a more honorable way. The corporate heads we had once trusted began stonewalling us, simply cutting off all communication in spite of the fact that the money they owed us was increasing.

At last, I took the problem to the medicine wheel. I was distressed at losing the money, of course; but what also bothered me was that someone I had once trusted had proved himself to be totally unworthy of that trust. In addition, I saw that the corporate tactics our associates were employing would cost perhaps as many as a hundred small companies like our own tens of thousands and, for some, hundreds of thousands of dollars. Legal counsel advised that, given their corporate protections, they were likely to get away with it!

I came to the wheel with much hope of finding a path to follow to a satisfactory resolution for all concerned, or at least to find a compromise where my own and others' injuries would be minimized. That day, the energy at the wheel was particularly high and very centered, which surprised me. The animals were holding their places, yet I felt no specific help forthcoming. If there was a message at all, it was that I should pay close attention to the fundamental teachings and the idiosyncratic character that each animal brought to the circle. As I began doing this, I found a sense of wholeness that was comforting. The agitation I was feeling over our business crisis was fading and a new plan was unfolding to move beyond it.

Then, as I was about to close that session, I checked in with Rabbit. I felt, rather than heard, his voice, which was the usual way I communicated with him, but his message was clear. In the weeks ahead I would encounter trials that would test me and teach me in new ways. I should be watchful. That is all Rabbit or any of the animals at the circle gave me that day.

The following afternoon I needed to get some books from the garage, which is under our house. I lifted the garage door, took two steps inside and stepped on a large rattlesnake! It instantly coiled and began rattling furiously.

At first I wasn't sure what it was. My eyes had not yet adjusted to the darkness but as they did, I saw the snake coiled and ready to strike, not three feet away. I quickly stepped away, outside its striking range, but then realized it was now between me and the outside door.

I watched for several minutes, spellbound not so much by the danger as by the beauty of this animal expressing its ultimate power. We stared at one another, awaiting the next move. The snake held its ground. I moved slightly and it moved in response, feigning a strike in my direction as if to warn me not to come closer. I sensed the animal's growing fear—along with my own, I might add—as the two of us recognized the potential gravity of the situation.

At first, I did not think about killing it. Instead I wondered how I was going to get it to go down to the woods, from whence I assumed it had come. Then I remembered hearing somewhere that rattlesnakes are very territorial. Chances are that it had come to the basement to hunt rodents, which meant that it considered this space its territory. I didn't like that concept at all. This was a place that Susan and I frequented in the course of doing our regular business. We stored our books and other printed material here. I had visions of Susan reaching for a box of books and surprising the snake. She was deathly afraid of rattlesnakes, so if she didn't get bitten she would be frightened at the very least.

Snake, I thought, *I regret this, but this is my territory and I am afraid I am going to have to kill you.*

I was not at all happy with this decision, nor was the rattler, who now retreated to a space behind some tools. It would be difficult to get it there, adding to my risk of getting bitten. I looked around for a weapon and spotted a hoe. I'll spare you the details, but after a considerable struggle I killed the snake. I sat with it as it died, sincerely mourning its demise rather than feeling triumphant. When it moved no more, I carried it down to a small cemetery near my medicine wheel where I have buried other animals that I have found dead on our property. I buried it next to an owl who met its end on the road near our house.

The snake visited my dreams for several days, and I brought the issue to the medicine wheel, too. I found myself thinking a lot about boundaries as they applied both to the snake and to the business associate who was cheating us. Was this the lesson the animal spirits spoke of? Whether they intended it or not I could not be certain, but it was an excellent lesson, one that continues to unfold, for the spirit of the snake now comes regularly to my circle.

Meanwhile, our business problems continued to escalate, and we began applying some of the lessons about protecting our boundaries that I had been learning from the incident with the snake. Even so, Susan and I were still incredulous about the behavior of our associates and so were continuing to seek ways to open communications with them and resolve some of the problems. It was very clear that they knew about boundaries; they were singularly focused on protecting their own, even if it meant bringing dozens of other companies down with them—pocketing money that was not theirs in the process. When I brought my concerns to the wheel, I got the clear message that I would not be able to adequately deal with this problem as long as I was unwilling to see the naked truth. These people had no compunctions at all about stealing from others or wrecking dozens of smaller companies for their own selfish gain.

I had yet another lesson to learn. In October, Susan went up to visit our grandchildren in Portland. The night after she left, I was awakened at two A.M. to the howl of what I knew was a mountain lion. It was close by, loud enough to awaken our two dogs, who, uncharacteristic of them, did not bark at the disturbance. Instead, they leapt up on the bed and snuggled close to me for protection.

Again I heard the howl, and realized it was coming from close to the medicine wheel. Then came another sound that troubled me even more, the mournful cry of an injured deer. Most people have never heard this cry. It is remarkably human in its expression of pain and fear and pathos. I couldn't just lay there listening to these horrible cries. I had to do something.

I leapt from bed, pulled on my clothes and boots, grabbed a flashlight and crept down the back steps to the woods. I heard, rather than saw, the big cat bounding off across the canyon to the east. It was apparently headed back toward Cow Mountain, a short distance away. I walked down the trail to the medicine wheel and shone the light around. Clearly, something had taken place here. The grass off the northern edge of the wheel—the position of Mountain Lion—was trampled down, showing that a struggle had taken place here. But if the big cat had made a kill, there was no carcass to be found.

I returned to the house, crawled back into bed, but could not go back to sleep for more than an hour. I thought about the cry of the deer and my thoughts naturally turned to the doe and her two fawns. I wanted to believe that somehow they were safe. Hopefully, I'd scared off the mountain lion before it could do them any harm.

Two days later, I was fixing myself some lunch. Something unusual caught my eye as I looked out the window above the kitchen sink. Beyond the gardens, sitting on our neighbor's fence post, was a huge black bird, a vulture, spreading its wings to dry them in the sun, as these carrion-eating creatures often do. This was a particularly large bird for our area, with a wingspan which I estimated at about six feet. Then I saw movement to the right of this bird. That image remains etched in my memory to this day: In a great sprawling oak tree there roosted ten or twelve dark figures—more vultures! I had never seen so many gathered in one place. They clung patiently to their roosts, all their attention riveted to a spot under the tree.

I left the house and went down to investigate. Intimidated by the huge birds, I crossed the field cautiously. Only a few yards from the tree, the vultures suddenly noted my approach and rose thunderously on their immense wings, only to settle into another tree thirty or forty yards down the hill. They were not about to leave. By then, my nose was already filled with the fetid air of rotting flesh.

I found the dead fawn near the fence line. It had been badly mauled by the mountain lion two nights before, and the vultures had begun to feast on the remains. I held a handkerchief to my nose, staring down at the gruesome figure, tears threatening as I remembered the doe parading her twins past the medicine wheel the first time. I thought about burying what was left of the corpse. But then I looked up and saw the vultures patiently waiting in the trees. Abhorrent though it was to me, it seemed right to let nature have her way, and leave the fawn's remains to these birds.

That evening I spent over an hour at the medicine wheel, meditating. I found that just being there, surrounded by the animal spirits, was calming and centering. Thirty yards away, the vultures shifted around restlessly in the trees, one or two occasionally dropping to the ground to take their share of the carrion.

It is difficult to verbalize what happened that day at the wheel. I had many questions, of course. Was this killing of the fawn intended as a lesson for me? More than likely, it was what Jung called "synchronicity," perhaps a coincidence, but perhaps part of a larger pattern that was beyond my understanding. It seemed more than coincidence that the doe had given birth to her twin fawns near the medicine wheel, and that the mountain lion had made its kill just a few feet from the northern quadrant, the position normally occupied by Mountain Lion at my wheel.

I went around the circle patiently, meditating several times on each animal, asking how they viewed what had happened here. There was, first and foremost, an acceptance of this event—the killing of the fawn. It was, after all, part of an order that they understood, or at least fully accepted. It was not until I was almost ready to leave that I remembered Rabbit, my power animal. I had not addressed it at all. I closed my eyes, and his image came into focus in my mind's eye. Here, to the best of my recollection, is the message I received from him that day:

Hunting and killing the fawn is just everyday behavior for the mountain lion in the wild. Deer are, after all, the mountain lion's natural prey. I should not judge this cycle of life being sacrificed for life in the wild because we humans are too far removed from it; we attribute values and morals to it that are of our own invention, and way off-track. Though this cycle exists for humans, too, we hide it from ourselves, and in the hiding we cause corruption and pain. We raise animals and butcher them for their meat but we sanitize the process. We grow crops and kill plants for our food. And so we remain blind to all the lessons we could learn of this cycle, and the dangers of the path we will take if we don't. Our self-imposed ignorance becomes a shadow cast over all our actions, creating misery for our fellow humans, as well as for the planet that supports and nurtures us.

Because we hide all this so successfully, we numb ourselves to truths that are required for living on the Earth. We hide from the cycle of life being sacrificed for life, and in time, what we do with these denied and repressed truths breeds indifference and fear and greed, making it easy to justify the annihilation, not only of other species, but our own species and whole ecosystems. Lost because we have blindfolded ourselves to these basic truths, we no longer enjoy the ecospiritual guidance offered us by animals and by the movements of planets in the cosmos and by the alchemy of the Earth. We forget who we are, and the terror of that lost wisdom haunts us.

With no guidance from these primary forces in our lives, a certain kind of insanity is born. It is driven by a stark indifference to spirit and by clinging to the physical and material world for solace that isn't available there. The insanity has now reached epic proportions, with huge corporations dominating the Earth, organizations peopled by millions who are no longer even aware of how far from the guidance of spirit and the natural world they have ventured. The corporations have become like giant creatures with minds of their own, who in their autonomy, have no allegiance even to those who nurture and support them. Guided by values evolving from technology, they have no conduit to the natural world, to the rhythms and cycles of the cosmos. It is easy for them to coldly sacrifice individuals or forests or whole nations for their own selfish gain.

Such are the lessons, Rabbit tells me, of Susan's and my entanglements with the business associates whose only guidance comes from the insane culture that their fear-driven world has created, a culture so separated from the higher order that it has no chance of surviving for long. The danger is that it can destroy far more than itself in the process of defending its own abstract existence. Unbeknownst to the hundreds of millions who serve and have come to depend on these cultures, their own quality of life is on a rapid descent, shored up by the short-lived excitement of gadgets and the latest electronic innovation.

The technological revolution has created an illusion that we have somehow subdued the cycle of life being sacrificed for life. We believe that we can at last make Nature do what we want her to do. We no longer have to fear the wilderness or our own mortality. Disconnected from the unseen reality of spirit, we cling to technology's illusions for comfort—yet part of us knows better. Like the soothing relief of a powerful drug these comforts fail to reach our souls. The fear, craziness, and bewilderment that results fuels the corporate culture's gross indifference to the life force, making it seem that the material rewards of modern technology are the only hope.

And what was the hope, then, for those of us who might seek ecospiritual guidance in our lives? Learn the lessons of the Wheel of Life, Rabbit answered. Learn from the diversity of spirit that the animals offer. Learn from Wolf about the spirit of nurturing and the importance of the continuum. Learn from Bear the spirit of standing in your own power through introspection and self-knowledge. Learn from Badger the spirit of honoring the survival instincts in each of us, even as you hold all life as precious. Learn to seek Mole's spiritual wisdom about the alchemy of the Earth. Learn the spirit of Mountain Lion's wisdom for tracking and seeking a higher truth. Learn from Eagle that living on the Earth is the spiritual lesson of your present life. And learn from your power animal that we humans have the capacity to look beyond what our five senses tell us and touch the unseen reality of the spirit.

The lessons of that week in my life continue to unfold. On a practical level, we have cut all our ties with the business associates I described, and have set in motion a plan to warn others about their unethical tactics. We are slowly forming an alternative vision of how to run that part of our business and the plan is moving forward quite nicely.

Meanwhile, with the help of the Wheel of Life, we are learning to trust the ecospiritual guidance offered by the animals.

7

The Metaphysics of the Wheel of Life

First culture was the flowering of human community based on the circle as the web of life. . . . What seems to have been intact in all these settings were the concentric circles of interconnection—the campfire, the extended family, the larger society, humanity, nature, and the mystery of Spirit.

—Christina Baldwin (1998)

Spirit, that which is the source of all and everything, is expressed in the circle. With no beginning, middle, or end, the circle speaks to us of unity. More than a symbol, it is an icon that projects our instinctive awareness of our oneness. The concept of oneness communicated in this way is simultaneously one of the first insights and one of the first puzzlements of human consciousness.

Circles and spirals painted or etched on the walls of caves, or formed on the ground with a gathering of rocks, and sculptures of human and animal figures arranged in circles, have been found throughout the world, some of them dating back to prehistoric times. The form of the circle has persisted in art, storytelling, music, dance, philosophy, and religion, even into present times, and all of these have early on been associated with rituals that celebrate our interconnectedness.

Our image of the Earth as seen from outer space is in the form of a circle. It is perhaps this recognition that fills us with excitement when we see this celestial image—part awe, part longing for our sense of oneness, and part appreciation of its mystery.

One of the first things spiritual teachers tell us is that we are one, that we exist in total unity with the cosmos. But what exactly does this mean? We can reason that the Universe is a unity and that each of us, in fact every living and inert thing with which we share this world, is part of this unity. We can intellectually grasp that everything we behold—ourselves, the trees, the ants, even the moon and stars—are one, yet can we truly experience it?

Our loss of spiritual connectedness often results in feelings of separation and isolation and fear. From the point at which we lose that connection, it is easy to believe that our very survival depends on our exploitation of the Earth and each other. Unless we are educated about what we are seeking on a deeper, spiritual level, these exploitative rationalizations are easy to justify in our minds. We become motivated by cultural slogans—survival of the fittest, convinced it is a dog eat dog world where me and mine come first, even at the risk of threatening the continuum of our own species. Soon we're surrounded by "me's" and "mine's" all competing for the same space and the same resources. Any dream of feeling our unity is displaced by further fear and

> *The Power of the world always works in circles, and everything tries to be round ... Even the seasons form a great circle in their changing, and always come back again to where they were. The life of a person is a circle from childhood to childhood, and so it is in everything where power moves.*
>
> —*Black Elk*

123

greed. The drive to escape scarcity has become a self-fulfilling prophecy and our worst fears have come true.

Unfortunately, we cannot experience our oneness until we have discovered the unity of experience within ourselves. Despite all the theories, we feel isolated from life as long as we feel divided within ourselves. Given the challenges of life and the nature of our egos, this inner unity is likely to be a long time in coming unless we develop skills to move beyond our illusions—and they are illusions—of separation and isolation. Early man recognized this and found a path to oneness through circle rituals—what I call in this book the wheel of life.

Circles of Individual Life

We humans have struggled with this issue of oneness for at least as long as recorded history. Greek mythology tells of a human creature who was both male and female, complete and whole, joined in a circle. But the gods, Zeus and Apollo, so feared this creature's power that they severed it in half. Presumably, by severing this creature into two—male and female—neither half would ever again experience its wholeness or its oneness with nature.

Though he did not necessarily subscribe to the Greek's view of the broken circle, Carl Jung dedicated his life to the exploration of individual wholeness and how to achieve it. During the middle of his life, he found himself creating small drawings and paintings within circles (mandalas). These images came spontaneously at first, rising out of his unconscious of their own volition. It was as if something within Jung's consciousness envisioned what he was seeking, and was pushing him to fully disclose it. He said of these drawings and paintings, "I saw the self—that is, my whole being—actively at work."

Based on the ubiquitous circle, these drawings suggested to their creator that each individual human consciousness is a microcosm orienting the person with the world around him. To Jung, each person's way of integrating their life experience was different, since the microcosm of their inner world was unique and would process whatever happened in its own way. The individual psyche was literally a world within a world, a wheel within a wheel. But Jung continued to have many questions: What held all the elements of the individual microcosm in place? What organized or directed it all?

Jung tells about a breakthrough dream he had which helped him complete his image of individual consciousness. He dreamed that he was visiting an island city. He had never been to this place before, and though he was aware of seeking some destination, he was not at all sure why he was there. As he made his way through the city, the streets were dark, and after much effort he found himself climbing a steep hill. Finally he reached the top where a huge tree was growing, surrounded by a luminescence which endowed it with exquisite beauty.

As he stood by the tree and looked out, he saw that the city had been designed in the shape of a wheel, with all the streets radiating out from the hub, the hill upon which Jung now stood, the center of it marked by the beautiful tree.

The unconscious helps by communicating things to us, or making figurative allusions. It has other ways, too, of informing us of things which by all logic we could not possibly know.

—C.G. Jung

When he awoke from this dream, Jung was ecstatic. He had just received the image of the human psyche that he had been seeking—the wheel with its organizing hub. So important was this dream to him that he split from Freud, his long-time associate and mentor, and moved on to pursue his own theories of personal development.

Based on the icon of the circle, Jung's exploration of the psyche moved from science and medicine, which had been his main references during his association with Freud, into Gnosticism, alchemy, and the Eastern spiritual traditions.

Wheels and transcendent imagery of unity appeared often in these disciplines, revealing human experience as a wheel within the larger continuum of the Universe.

As his work progressed, veering dramatically away from Freud's influence, Jung discovered mystical sources that were integral parts of human growth. He experienced first-hand how spirit helpers can rise of their own volition from within the psyche—helpers which were not products of his personality. They existed independently of him and had a body of experience all their own. Their presence in his inner world lent much to his expanding knowledge about the path to wholeness. There seemed no question that human consciousness had access to sources of knowledge beyond physical existence.

During this time, Jung met, through his friend Mahatma Gandhi, a man whose personal guru had been dead for several centuries. The man explained to Jung that, "Most people have living gurus. But there are always some who have a spirit for a teacher." (Jung 1965)

In one of Jung's earliest writings, "Septem Sermones ad Mortuos," he drew upon the teachings of Basilides, who lived in the second century A.D. Basilides described the nature of the Universe and the concept of oneness. He spoke of the Pleroma, which included both the physical world and what had existed before it. He said, "because we are parts of the Pleroma, the Pleroma is also in us. Even in the smallest point is the Pleroma endless, eternal, and entire, since small and great are qualities which are contained in it" (ibid, app. V).

Within the view of the self which Jung gives us, any sense of separation we might experience has to be of our own creation, an illusion. But illusion or not, it can impede our growth and limit how we relate to the world. The most important part of this insight is that just because we don't feel our oneness does not mean it doesn't exist. These feelings do not control or determine the nature of the Universe after all. Given that, experiencing our oneness might be as simple as taking responsibility for the part we play in creating the illusion, and then tricking ourselves into seeing beyond it. This is the everyday magic with which we free ourselves from all our illusions, so why not this one?

The Parliament of Fowls

I have always found it curious that Jung never made mention of the fourteenth century author, Geoffrey Chaucer, whose long poem titled "The Parliament of Fowls," would have surely been of interest to him. While this is an obscure work by that author, who is best known for his *Canterbury Tales*, a person of Jung's broad education would probably have been familiar with it. Had he been, it would have been a good example of how individuals relate to a larger whole, as demonstrated by a council circle. (It is also an example of learning from the animals.)

Chaucer's poem tells the story of the falcon, the king of the birds. One day, he announces to his kingdom that his son has come of age and it is time for him to find a partner. Falcon orders all the birds to gather around and hold council to help the young prince choose a worthy mate. And so the circle is formed, with every bird in the kingdom eagerly participating, convinced that he or she has the ultimate answer for the young prince.

After some ceremony, the young falcon comes and takes his place at the circle, promising to listen carefully to the counsel that is to be given him. The circle comes alive with excitement and the falcon king appoints one of the birds to begin. Each bird in turn will have its say, he explains, and each will be treated as an equal. At the end, young falcon will announce his choice.

As each bird expounds on the qualities the young falcon should seek in a mate, we quickly see that each one is drawing this advice from the perspectives of their own life experience. The duck, for example, exalts the qualities of a mate with webbed feet while the swan glorifies the mate with powerful wings and a long graceful neck. Through it all, the falcon king and his son listen patiently, seeking the wisdom that each one of the birds offers. By the end, the reader knows quite well what Chaucer is doing. He is commenting on the nature of human knowing: That we each tend to filter our impressions of life through idiosyncratic lenses, molded from who we are and what we have experienced.

When all the birds have had their turn, the young falcon is asked to speak, to tell what he has learned. He thanks all the birds for speaking so eloquently and assures them that their speeches have indeed been valuable to him, revealing exactly what he must do. He tells them that while each of them spoke of the benefits of different qualities, they all shared a common message with him that he would take to heart. This message was that, in the choice of a mate, there could be small differences in manner and temperament, but in the final analysis there were immutable attributes in both oneself and one's potential mate that had to be honored since they were of a higher law than any single one of them could claim. In choosing a mate, as elsewhere in life, we must be true to ourselves. Then young falcon described what he would seek in a mate, naming all the attributes of the same species as himself. In the end, a chorus of bird voices rose up, celebrating the young falcon's choice.

We might draw parallels between this and other councils, from contemporary ones to ones dating back to paleolithic times. It would be easy to imagine stories similar to this being acted out in the caves at Lascaux, twelve thousand years ago, as Cro-Magnon men and women gathered there to pay homage to the spirits of animals and the Source that created them. Though the language would have been different, there is a very real possibility that they counseled around the circle and treated this form as an icon rich in meaning. Maybe the paintings of animals on the walls of the cave had a part in all this, helping Cro-Magnon people ponder their relationships with each other and the infinite cosmos.

Leaping Past the Circle of Our Illusions

Because it has no beginning, middle, or end, the circle challenges our obsession with finite thinking. As physical beings, we seek explanations that can be contained within at least a beginning and an end. We want to be assured that we know, that we can, using our finite minds, somehow hold and maybe even control life. Yet, if we gaze long enough into space, we cannot help but notice that we are living in a universe with no beginning, middle, or end. We do our best to describe this infinite universe in finite terms—since that is all we have to work with—but such efforts are always doomed to failure. And so we salve our egos with theories of how it all began, bypassing the fact that we can't describe how something that had no beginning got started. Physicists and cosmologists tell us that our universe began with the Big Bang, which was the explosion of the cosmic egg which contained all the elements of matter from which our world and everything else was made. What they can't explain is the primal source of that stuff contained in the cosmic egg. No one thinks to ask, "Whose cosmic chicken laid that egg?"

What it comes down to is this: Instead of trying so hard to solve the mystery of mysteries, let's bask in it instead. We've forgotten how to do that. It's the essence of spirituality, fostering awe, reverence, gratitude, and humility.

The Wheel of Life teachings that have been in existence for at least as far back as paleolithic times, allow us to do just that—bask in the mystery. These sacred rituals provide the opportunity to recognize the part we play in creating our illusions of separation. We can gather as friends, business associates, or community members around these wheels— some call them "council circles"—to seek answers to difficult questions. The circle sets the stage for us to trick ourselves into seeing beyond our own limited, individual perceptions. When the powers of the council circle are working, their magic carries us into and beyond the finite truths of our individual lives, bringing us face to face with the infinite truths of our oneness.

As often as not, this moment of oneness is fleeting, yet, as with any epiphany, it can be life-changing. In workshops where we have gathered in council circles, I have seen this happen again and again. The experience might begin by simply creating the safe setting where people can speak their own truths from the heart. Each participant is encouraged to reach into the memories of their own life experience and share that experience with the others at the circle. They might share a personal wound, a victory, or a moment of ecstasy. The challenge is to tell this story from a place of total personal integrity, not to impress or entertain, but just to share the experience in the most engaging way possible.

When each individual truth is shared in this way, a stillpoint emerges. The stillpoint is experienced as we reach a quiet place in our minds, one that is like a placid mountain stream, a place in our consciousness that is undisturbed by our individualized perceptions and interpretations. When two or more at the circle touch this place, the experience swiftly spreads around the circle. As our minds quiet, we hear what the young falcon heard, the universal message hidden behind our individual differences. We see our own individual truths more clearly. The importance of the individual's microcosm of truth is acknowledged, with all its contradictions. But we also see its limits, and are at least momentarily at peace with them, compassionate toward ourselves and others. In light of this knowledge, our illusions dissolve and we open to a greater Truth—a Truth with a capital "T." We see, among other things, that this greater Truth is a collective effort. We cannot achieve it alone. The council circle teaches us to see how interdependent we are, and in this interdependence we create a collective lens through which we may find our inner and outer oneness.

I am reminded here of a story told to me by a Kiowa Indian friend who grew up on the reservation. The U.S. government imposed their values on them, undermining the old ways. He said that his maternal grandfather, who was the chief of the tribe, spoke of "the time before the white government's fences and money, along with their emphasis on the nuclear family instead of on the collective strength of the tribal circle, had destroyed the old ways." Prior to this, he explained, there was a belief that all beings were joined as one in a sacred circle. There was even an understanding that one's enemies were part of that sacred circle, and it was only the limits of individual thought that caused them to see each other as adversaries. Even with this compassionate perspective, two neighboring tribes could be locked in these adversarial positions for generations. Contradictions of this kind were not questioned. They were seen as part of life and were accepted until wisdom revealed a better way.

Beyond these contradictions, a higher truth prevailed, and this was the belief that all Mother Earth's creations should share in any abundance that any one of them enjoyed. If one tribe was lucky in a hunt and killed many buffalo, and they heard that their neighbor was hungry, it was their duty to make certain that the neighbor was fed, even if that neighbor was an enemy. It was understood that the buffalo were the gift of the Great Spirit and were for the benefit of all "two-leggeds." Making war was the business of men; feeding people was the business of the Great Spirit. It was important to keep these priorities straight, honoring the Great Spirit above one's own wishes or presumptions. Enemies fed enemies, even though the following day they might be fighting again. Here was evidence that, while we might be compelled to follow the path of our individual truths, there was a higher Truth, based on the great circle of oneness, that had to be honored.

Forming Circles in Your Life

Council circles have been in existence from as far back as we can determine—tens of thousands of years—and they still exist and are taken very seriously by many people the world over. Even more powerful than silent meditation, the circle can direct us back to our sense of connectedness and oneness.

It is a way of thinking that each of us can bring into our lives, and by so doing the way in which we relate to ourselves and the world around us will be changed for the better. This doesn't necessarily mean that we should immediately call all our friends and business associates into council together, though I would submit that this would do much to heal the diseases and wounds of our planet. But by beginning to integrate the insights and the practice of the circle into our lives we move closer to experiencing our own oneness and bringing the wisdom of this experience into our everyday lives.

When most of us use the word "council," we usually think of a roomful of politicians and experts brought together to resolve a conflict or make a group decision. If your concept of making council happens to be associated with Indians, you might even have an image of a bunch of people with feathered war bonnets sitting around smoking a long, strange-looking pipe and deciding to make war or peace, as the case may be. Apropos of this, a few summers ago, I spoke with a Navajo man who was raised in San Diego, where his parents were in the military. He told about his first trip to visit his aunt and uncle in Arizona when he was six years old. When he was told that his uncle was going to a council meeting at the reservation one night, the boy became very upset. Noting this, his aunt asked him what was wrong. My friend told her that he had learned all about councils in cowboy and Indian movies, and it meant that the Indians were going to go on the warpath . . . and he wanted to go home!

So it is not just those of us from European-American descent who might be confused about these terms. In its own inimitable way, Hollywood has created truths that never existed outside the film directors' minds.

Specific rituals associated with the council circle vary greatly from one nation of people to another, and from one continent to another. Sometimes circles are called for special circumstances, such as births, deaths, or for healing a community problem, and each of these may have its own form. Finally, the person calling the circle may have a specific way that he or she runs it. Even with the great variations one might encounter, there are some qualities that are sacred and always observed:

First, the core purpose of calling the circle is to honor all living things and to remember that, regardless of our species, our station in life, our age, gender or race, we are all spirit and all come from the same source.

As we sit at the wheel, we may appear different on the surface. We may speak different languages, have very different ways of life, associate ourselves with different political parties, and even vehemently disagree on certain issues. But by virtue of sharing the common spirit of life, we are all equals while we sit at the circle. We are not here to prove anything about our own views of life.

Second, our goal at the circle is to listen as equals and acknowledge the importance of each person, or other beings, who may joins us. If animals are present, they must be acknowledged. Spirit teachers, either animal or human, may also join, and should be acknowledged.

The Circle is a sacred reminder of the interrelationship, respect, and clarity that come from opening oneself up to the energy of the Circle of Life—the wisdom offered by one's experiences, the experiences of others, and the world in which we live. The Circle is a sacred symbol reminding us of the importance of our unique place in the Universe and our relationship to all things.

—Michael Garrett

When a circle is held where wild or domestic animals share the environment, it is my belief that the human participants should be prepared to acknowledge and welcome these brothers and sisters into the circle.

I have participated in a number of circles held in wilderness areas in New Mexico. Surrounded by thousands of acres of open land, the animals are more populous than humans, and they often make their presence known at our circles. In the midst of a lightning storm, a mountain hummingbird joined one of our circles, whistling at the window of the yurt where we were meeting, singing with the drum that was part of the opening ceremony that stormy night. Three of the twenty human participants later told how, for many years, their own spirit helpers had been hummingbirds. No one has yet explained to me why any self-respecting hummingbird would have ventured out on that dark, stormy night to sing at our circle.

On another occasion, Raven tapped on our window and cawed, letting his presence be known even as one of the participants was telling a story about this bird. Still another time, as my wife Susan was telling how horses inspired her to seek her own creative power, we heard hoofbeats rapidly approaching. An instant later, a magnificent mare galloped into the clearing in front of our meeting place and danced for us as we watched. The odd thing was that in the four or five years we'd been meeting there, we had never seen a horse on this ranch. She had escaped from a neighbor's corral nearly a mile away. Her wonderful dance for us left little doubt in our minds that we should always leave space in our lives for serendipitous meetings with animals, humans, and spirits of all species. Rather than treating their appearances as interruptions or coincidences these surprise visits should be given the same quality of attention given to anyone else at the circle.

Where to Start

You might call a circle for any reason. A group of neighbors might come together at the circle to share their feelings about a problem arising in their community. Parents might come together to share their feelings concerning the challenges of parenting. When a community crisis occurs, people might come together at the circle to share their stories and provide support. A group might be called to talk about spiritual matters and explore the possibility of starting a regular group to meet in that way. The gathering might begin with the sharing of a meal, with people getting introduced, and friends catching up on each others' news. This relaxed, convivial atmosphere brings people together in an informal way, and sets the tone of the gathering.

The facilitator then calls for the circle to come together. It is good to be prepared so that people can enter a room where the right number of chairs are set out in the circle, or where there are pillows on the floor for sitting. At the center of the circle you might have a small table, carpet, or piece of decorative fabric. A candle, spiritual object, photo of something meaningful to the group or that highlights the meaning for the gathering that day might be placed there.

I feel that it is important to keep a tone that is real and convivial, and to be careful not to weigh down the circle with religious or spiritual iconography. Keep in mind that the purpose of the circle is to encourage people to speak from the heart, and to feel free to do this in their own way, without the pressure of having to conform to a standard that is unfamiliar to them. I've participated in circles that were so heavily endowed with the facilitator's own "spiritual stuff" that only those who were already comfortable with this were able to speak. The most active circles have been those which were down to earth, honoring the fact that participants might be from a variety of religious and ethnic backgrounds which had their own icons and rituals.

As people choose and take their places at the circle, it helps to have some kind of ritual to settle people down and bring them together. My own preference is to have simple rhythm instruments available, such as a hand drum or two, some simple rattles, sticks to click together, and so on. Be sure to explain this to any new group beforehand, being light about it as you tell them that it is a way of bringing the energy of the circle together. Some people are not comfortable with such instruments, usually because they do not feel they can carry a beat. That's okay. Participation is strictly voluntary. Usually about a third to half of any group will drum or rattle, and that is more than enough to center the energy.

Another way to bring the energy together is with a silent meditation lasting up to a minute and a half. Depending on the group, the leader might offer a prayer or a personal statement that dedicates the circle to a specific purpose.

I like to use a talking stick when the talking actually begins. A talking stick can be any object that can be comfortably held in the hand. Usually it is made of wood, decorated in ways that express something about its use. The leader should explain that whoever holds the talking stick has the right to speak. Others at the circle are to give the person with the talking stick their full attention. Others may ask questions or make comments only with the permission of the person holding the stick.

Usually the leader of the group is the first to hold the stick. She or he might begin with a statement about why the circle was called, acknowledging anyone else who has helped. It is good to use some humor at this time, not necessarily by telling a joke (unless it really illustrates this moment), but perhaps by sharing something from your own life that lets everyone loosen up. Keep the focus on the circle, however, and remember that you are not there to entertain but to encourage people to speak from their hearts.

I like to make it clear to people that the power of the circle is not in the ritual itself, but in what the people themselves bring to it. If it's a new circle meeting for the first time, this is a good time to explain the rules of the game, as it were. Participants will be passing the talking stick around the circle in a clockwise direction. In the first pass, each person who holds the stick simply introduces her- or himself, telling briefly what brought them here. When all people present have introduced themselves, the talking stick is passed again. This time, whoever holds the stick at any given moment shares their feelings about the issue that has brought the circle together. Comments are kept very personal, and people are encouraged to speak from the "I" point of view.

This process is not easy for everyone. In most schools, we are taught that our personal opinions and feelings are of little value. If we write a paper or give a speech about an event in history, for example, any personal points of view must be "validated" with quotes of "experts," people who know what they are talking about—and that would certainly not include you! In introducing people to the circle, you might point this out and tell them that here, what we feel and what we have experienced firsthand is the top priority.

No arguments, recommendations, criticisms, advice, or solutions are to be offered or expected here. This may be the most difficult thing for people who have never before participated in a talking circle to understand. We are a culture of "helpers," always ready to offer our wisdom or aid. Doing so is the best way to squelch the power and magic of the circle. It may take people a while to catch on, but they will after experiencing the power of the circle.

After three or four passes around the circle, the talking stick may be placed in the center. Whoever wants to speak after that will go to the center and pick it up, then return to her or his place at the circle to say his or her piece.

When everyone has spoken who wants to speak, it is time to close the circle. Preface the closing ceremonies by telling people that everything said should stay in the circle, that talking about it with people who were not at the circle is not advised. Of course, in the days ahead, people who were at the circle may wish to have further discussion with one or more of the others who were there, and that is encouraged.

The circle is now closed with a statement, or perhaps a prayer, that captures the tone and collective message that emerged. As they depart, it is suggested that if possible, people spend some quiet time, perhaps meditating, to allow the experience of the circle to sink in.

In the beginning, you may find that people go away wondering what they are supposed to do with whatever happened at the circle. Most, however, will begin to have little breakthroughs of recognition in the days or weeks ahead.

When you have called a circle to address a problem—a community or school problem, for example—an action group might emerge from the circle. That's fine, of course, and their meetings would follow their own agendas and rules. Meanwhile, the talking circle is maintained as described above.

For more on working with circles, I highly recommend Christina Baldwin's fine book on this subject, *Calling the Circle: The First and Future Culture.*

8
Daily Practice

> *"Everything I've put you through,"* don Juan
> told Castaneda, *"each of the things I've shown
> you was only a device to convince you that there's
> more to us than meets the eye. . . . "* Learning
> involves a change in behavior. . . . It's not
> enough to accumulate new thoughts; you must be
> able to act, to do . . .
>
> —Ken Eagle Feather

The animals are all around us, all the time, be it a single hummingbird in our garden, the family dog, a mountain lion on a trail we have taken into the wilderness, or even the mice in the basement. We share this planet with them, be it the nearby fields and wetlands, the skies above our heads, the forests that encircle us, or beneath the ground that supports us. The awesome beauty of these creatures touches us in ways that we are hard-pressed to describe, and in their absence we feel hollow.

I remember a fishing trip into the Sierras that I made with a friend several years ago. We camped near a rapidly flowing river, and ventured forth the following morning, fly rods in hand, to test our skill at the fisher's art. We waded the river for most of the day, but after not raising a single bite in all that time, I sat down on a stump to contemplate my surroundings. Something wasn't right, and I could not immediately put my finger on what it was. I felt restless and troubled.

My friend finally caught up with me. He was depressed. "I don't get it," he said. "I haven't seen a thing all day."

And then I realized what had been bothering me. It wasn't the lack of fish. It was nothing. I mean, literally that: nothing. There had been no sign of any life along the stream. Not only were there no fish, there were no bugs, no frogs, no snakes, no birds, no rabbits, no squirrels. Nothing!

We walked back to our camp and when I spotted a forest ranger I stopped him and asked, "What's going on? We were out along the stream all day and we didn't see a single fish."

"Oh," he said, "this is only Wednesday. They won't bring the fish in until tomorrow afternoon." He explained that in the morning, the Department of Fish and Game would dump a truckload of trout from the hatchery at the bridge a few miles upstream. He looked at my fly rod. "You won't catch much with that, though. Salmon eggs are best." He explained that because of the way they were fed from the day they were hatched, the young trout didn't recognize bugs or flies as food. And because they sprayed in this area to keep the bug population down, there wasn't much in the way of real bugs to entice the trout and teach them that bugs were a food source.

"That explains why there are so few birds and reptiles," I added, noting that these animals, too, depended on the bugs for their sustenance.

The ranger looked at me blankly, as if he'd never thought of this. "I guess you're right," he said.

My friend and I packed up our gear and drove home silently, cutting our trip short by three days. This certainly wasn't what we'd planned. We talked about it on the way down, realizing that we had not come to the wilderness just to fish. We'd come for the unexpected, to be surprised by encounters with other beings, to be reminded of the water walker, to hear the calls of birds seldom heard in the city, to possibly encounter a family of raccoons by the river at night, to spot a bear or two in the distance, to watch dragon flies skimming the surface of the stream. Here, at an elevation over 7,000 feet, they'd sanitized the wilderness, turned it into a safe and sterile playground where weekend fishermen could hook captive fish, specially bred just for them, by tossing hooks of fluorescent-dyed salmon eggs into the water. We wondered how many other people came to this place each year, then went away slightly troubled and disappointed but unable to put their fingers on what had been wrong. Or were there those whose goals were so singularly focused on catching a few fish by whatever means that they didn't notice what was missing? More than ever, situations like this should not only surprise, but alarm us.

There is so much to be gained by quieting our minds and observing our fellow creatures; only then can we receive as much as they have to teach us. This is not always easy because we want them to be like us, and we want to feel we are in control of them. The bonds we and our family pets develop, for example, are often the result of our projecting human attributes to them—they know when we are unhappy or sad. They seem at times to read our minds, or to be doing things for the same reasons that we would do them. How easy it is to see what we want to see in them, to *anthropomorphize* them, and in the process, rob them of who they really are. The crime, then, is that we may miss what they have to teach us. Most of us are aware of learning from our pets, of course, but how often we miss their greatest gifts to us! I love the following example, since it was the first time I fully realized the depth of the spiritual influence our family animals can have in our daily lives.

When my wife Susan and I first got together, some fourteen years ago, she had a big yellow cat named Tigger. At first, Tigger didn't like me at all. He would force his way between us in bed. He would stalk me at night, and bite or claw at my bare feet. And he guarded the phone, laying across it and swatting at me with his sharp claws, preventing me from touching it. I was the only person in the family he treated that way. This was his territory and he made it clear that I was an interloper. He was clearly the alpha male and wanted me to know it.

In time, Tigger and I made our peace. He didn't like me touching him, not even affectionately, but he at least accepted me enough to sit beside me and press gently against my thigh as I read. But perhaps the biggest lesson he taught me had to do with his relationship with Susan. Soon after she and I got together, we faced a number of serious health problems and family problems. At the height of our joy at finding each other, everything else in our lives was coming apart at the seams. But I noticed that when Susan got upset, she would retreat to her room to think things over. I would find her in bed with Tigger purring contentedly on her chest. Almost magically, Tigger's purring (he purred very loudly!) seemed to center and ground Susan. The animal rhythms communicated in the vibration against his mistress' rib cage and heart, nearly always succeeded in bringing Susan into a place of clarity and resolve. Even after Tigger died, at the ripe old age of fourteen, Susan was able to center herself in the midst of travail, just as Tigger had taught her to do.

Did Tigger consciously pass along this lesson? I doubt it, though I have to admit that he was tenacious in serving this role whenever he sensed Susan's upset. But that is not the point, nor is it a question we can answer with any certainty. The animals teach us unselfconsciously. Mostly, I don't think they are in any way motivated to change us or pass lessons on to us. That may, in fact, be their greatest gift to us—that they stand in their own power, expressing the direction they receive from that ultimate source whose mutual relationship we all share. It is up to us to observe their lessons and receive whatever meaning they offer us.

Recently, my friend Ken Eagle Feather, told me about a large buck deer who literally ran into the side of his car as he was driving home one evening. This collision between machine and animal caused considerable damage to the car and unknown damage to the deer. The latter ran off into the woods.

Ken asked what I thought that lesson might have meant. Is there an answer that is not simply a projection of our own belief systems? Probably not, since we have trouble seeing beyond our own projections even with our fellow humans. But it certainly begs repeating a lesson that I received at my medicine wheel some years ago.

I learned that there is a kind of graduated hierarchy of animals that defines the boundaries between the wilderness home of the animals and the manicured symmetry of human civilization. This hierarchy extends from the wildest—those animals we seldom see to those who actually share our homes with us. Some, like dogs and cats, have become so humanized that they will seek the company of their human companions above members of their own species, even chasing off the latter if they come too close. We share an intimacy with our pets that acts as a reminder, and sometimes as a bridge, between our own species and others.

Horses and other domesticated animals have been brought into the human world, too, serving us in various ways, and certainly not all of these relationships are fair or ennobling for anyone involved. In any case, these creatures are a step further away from our lives. But then we start moving further up the hierarchy toward the wild and rare. Depending on what we leave untouched in the natural landscape, or provide for in other ways, there are the song birds, the crows, ravens, and owls. They are certainly more wild than our cats and dogs, but they may also learn to live fairly harmoniously with us, even while keeping their distance. The same goes for squirrels and chipmunks.

Next come the deer. Even in the suburbs we may encounter deer, who have enough trust of humans to wander into their gardens and nibble at the sweet and colorful flowers the two-leggeds plant. But the deer are special; they are boundary markers, creatures who are more wild than domestic. They learn to make use of the gardens that humans cultivate, but are not ready to submit to human controls. Along this same boundary between the wilderness and civilization, we may encounter raccoons, skunks, and opossums. The next level away from the human world, and toward the wilderness, are animals such as bears, who have learned to raid garbage dumps, camper's stashes of food, and even coolers left in the back of travelers' cars, peeling off the doors as we would peel an orange.

As we get much further into the wild we may encounter rarer cats, such as bobcats, ringtailed cats, and even mountain lions. Here, too, are the rarer birds such as bald eagles and condors and certain rare breeds of owls. Snakes and slithery creatures become more common, too, the further we range beyond the pavement. And in the furthest reaches are increasingly wilder creatures, and primordial creatures whose ancestors inhabited the earth long before the energy of life took human form. In distant jungles we find rhinos, elephants, pythons, howler monkeys, gorillas and zebra—all creatures so wild they have little or no tolerance for us two-leggeds.

It is the deer who mark the line between our two worlds. At the place in our world where they appear in our gardens, or run into the sides of our cars, or lay dead in the ditches where they have been killed by our cars—this is an important marker for us. It is a place where we first encounter a decision, a question, about what our relationship to them is. Presumably, we are more conscious, more aware of our choices than they. Presumably, we recognize the dangers to them when they come too close to us. Presumably, we can reflect on what these boundaries mean to us and to them, and make wise choices about how far to press into their spaces—and what the expense of this infiltration of their boundaries means to both of us. Presumably!

Do we really understand what the animals give us, what they are doing in our world? Do we really understand the value of having diverse creatures on this planet? Why do they come to us in our dreams? Why do they visit our environment with their purring, with their songs, with their graceful dances over meadows and ranges? What have we lost in the way of the human cultures that four generations back based an entire way of life around the buffalo, or the deer, or the wolf? These were cultures based on the primal truths of living on a planet that their shamans had somehow viewed from the heavens, or from a vantage point that allowed them to revere the relationship they had with Her— with Mother Earth, the Pachamama. Their spiritual insights came from being able to traverse beyond the boundaries of singularly human existence to enter the world of animals and, in the process, discover the unseen reality of the spirit.

We must be particularly careful about those boundaries where the deer appear suddenly in the beams of our headlights, and where squirrels rattle around in the rafters of our homes. We must at those places ask essential questions, such as how much deeper into the wilderness we dare go before we encounter the creatures higher on the wilderness pyramid? When we go much farther beyond the deer, we encroach on those who, like the mountain lion, have little or no tolerance for us. They will stand and fight, knowing that the survival of their own species depends on defending their territory and winning. And we must learn to have the good sense to back away, to recognize the danger to all of us if we press deeper into this other world.

To have personal power animals, to work with the lessons of the animals at the medicine wheel, to ask what are perhaps unanswerable questions about why the animals are here with us—all this is important. Any spiritual system that excludes other species not only isn't honoring the rights of other creatures, is also failing to honor Creation itself. Remember, God ordered Noah to bring the animals aboard his ark when the great floods came. Apparently, our Creator

considered them important. Shouldn't we take that message as seriously as Noah did? There is much to learn about ourselves from the animals, not the least of which is our own arrogance and what we must learn to master in ourselves so that we can learn to become responsible caretakers of our planet.

It is odd to think that modern man had to invent multibillion dollar spaceship programs to gain the perspective of our planet that ancient peoples instinctively realized tens of thousands of years ago. It remains to be seen what we will do with the knowledge we have gained from these missions beyond our mother planet—whether we will take our technological achievements as a sign that we can conquer the Universe or whether the imagery it has provided will direct us back inward, where we are humbled by the mystery of Creation and touched by its beauty and love.

I am quite certain that, as long as we are willing to open ourselves to the lessons of the animals, we have a chance of rediscovering the wonder and profound pleasures of simply basking in the mysteries of Creation. I am quite certain we can stop fearing it and rest in its bounty. But this will take daily practice, a constant awareness, reminded of this larger vision and greater mission each time we hear the song of a bird, or catch the burning eyes of some wild creature peering at us through the bright beams of our headlights on a dark evening's journey.

Smudging

Smudging is the process of spiritually cleansing or clearing an area by burning a fragrant herb, usually sage mixed with cedar, heather, or sweetgrass. The herbs are burned in a small earthenware pot, or sometimes in an abalone shell, fanned over the area where you are working with your hands or a feathered fan.

When working with a large medicine wheel, I like to go all the way around the circle, holding the burning smudge and fanning it gently as I go. I may go around the circle as many as three or four times. I stop at each of the four directions, fanning the smoke away from my body while bringing to mind all that I associate with that direction. This is always done in the spirit of gratitude for what I have learned, and am still to learn, from that position at the wheel.

At each of the six directions, plus the center, I call to mind a mental image of the animal who guards that space, thanking them—aloud or in my mind—while smudging them as I would a person. As you become familiar with the smudging ritual, you will develop your own style for doing it. If you have a teacher who recommends a specific way of doing it, do it that way with the understanding that what ultimately gives any ritual its power is the balance between honoring the original intent and finding a way of performing the ritual that speaks to you and accesses the wisdom you bring to it.

The smudging ceremony has been used for as far back as we can find records in human history. Versions of the same basic principles have been found worldwide, and in every tradition from Celtic to Roman Catholic. It is a way to create a space for new knowledge and change.

The principle of smudging is literally that we are clearing the air and preparing for something new or unusual to be observed or practiced. As such, it is important for those of us who are performing the ritual, as well as for those partaking of it, to acknowledge and honor the principles and to participate as fully as we can.

Undoubtedly the most important principle is that smudging is like drawing a curtain between everyday life and this moment. In smudging, we are saying, I acknowledge that, at this moment, I am entering a different space than my everyday life. I will do what I can to leave the beliefs and limitations of my everyday life behind me and participate as openly as I can in whatever this special time has to offer me. As the smudging ritual is performed, imagine that all that is of your everyday life is being carried off in the smoke, and that the scent of the smudging material is preparing this new space. Note that there is nothing magical in the smoke or scent itself (i.e., the benefits come only to those who participate with their hearts and minds). The power of the ritual lies in your ability to quiet yourself inwardly, and allow the smoke and scent of the smudge to create this temporary separation from your everyday life and this preparation of the coming moment in you.

What You Will Need

1. Dried herbs such as sage. These are usually available at any stores that carry ceremonial supplies. Try metaphysical bookstores and Native American supply stores. The

sage comes in a "smudge stick," which is a tight bundle of herbs tied together with a bit of string or yarn. White sage, which is particularly fragrant, comes as loose leaves.

2. A small, fireproof pot or abalone shell to hold the ashes. This can be as modest as the terra cotta saucer for a flower pot.

3. A fan (optional). You can easily make one by tying together three large feathers at the quill.

4. Matches or a cigarette lighter.

Some Basic Principles to Observe:

1. If you are allergic to the smoke, you may want to just wave the herbs around without burning them, using the aromatic qualities of the herbs to cleanse the area without the smoke. If you are a participant in a ceremony where someone is smudging, and you are sensitive to the smoke, tell them that the smoke bothers you, and ask them to hold it away from you so that you do not have to breathe it directly. Sometimes, if the person is smudging with a feathered fan, they will smudge the fan, then wave it around you without as much smoke. As with any ritual or ceremony, it is the power in the intention that is important.

2. As you are smudging, you and any participants should try to silence your minds as much as possible, just as you would if you were meditating. There should be no talking at this time, and the process should be observed by everyone in the room. As one person is being smudged (or is smudging her/himself), all in the room should be holding that same energetic space—letting the smoke carry away thoughts of the everyday world as the scent of the smudge prepares the present space.

3. A smudge stick or a scented candle may be substituted in this ritual. Even a jar of aromatic herbs or dried flower petals may be employed, with or without burning. Similarly, while a feathered fan is nice to have, the fanning process may just as well be performed with the hands.

4. The way I was taught to smudge was to smudge from the front of the body, beginning near the pelvis (base) and working up, to the head, then out of the top of the head (crown chakra). This can be accomplished with a fairly rapid but gentle fanning, moving the smoke (or simply the air) up and beyond the body. If you are familiar with the chakras, you may imagine the smudge moving through them, and in the process you are reminding yourself of the importance of each chakra center in the personal evolution of the person.

5. Understand that the "magic" or power of the smudging is in the strength and purity of the intent, held in the minds of both the person who performs the smudging and the person receiving it.

6. There are infinite ways to perform this ceremony. One way is for one person to smudge as the other receives the smudge, with both holding the intent of creating the separation from everyday life and the preparation of the coming moment. Another way is for the smudge and fan (or scented candle, or simply fan) to be passed around the circle for each person to partake of on their own.

7. Keep the ritual simple and light, always reminding yourself of the importance of your own intent.

8. Close with a moment of gratitude for your knowledge of this useful ritual and for the gifts of nature (sage, fire, air, etc.) that make it possible. This can be done silently.

APPENDIX B

A Veterinarian Reflects on Human-Animal Relationships

C. S. Manette, D.V.M.

Author's Preface to the Appendix

About the time that I finished the first draft of this book, a friend who was just graduating from veterinary school shared the following paper with me. I was deeply moved. I had never fully recognized the role of veterinarians in our society. My experience with them had been limited to those rare occasions when I had taken a family pet to a clinic for shots or to check up on an injury or illness. My friend's paper, however, reminded me that as physicians veterinarians are at the forefront of human-animal relationships. They witness how we relate to the animals, and they must struggle each day—sometimes consciously, sometimes unconsciously—with their own personal mythologies and beliefs around the roles we and the animals play in each others' lives.

While my friend's paper is presented in a very different tone than the rest of this book, it addresses key issues about our evolving relationships with animals that needed to be included. Dr. Manette's work goes way beyond addressing the ethics of veterinary medicine, asking, as James Hillman did, questions that may ultimately determine our own survival in the century ahead: What is our relationship with the animals? Why, throughout the ages, have they populated our dreams and our mythologies? Our relationships with the animals can teach us a lot about ourselves and the mysteries of life and death, unveiling issues that we perhaps can answer no other way.

When, according to the Bible, God ordered Noah to build an ark and fill it with two of each species, He must have had something in mind. It was no accident that this planet was to be populated not just with our own species but with seemingly infinite ones. With untold species disappearing each day, most of them the result of human activities, it is more important than ever to ask what God might have had in mind when He issued these orders to Noah. Dr. Manette's paper doesn't answer that question, any more than this book does. But it certainly probes more deeply into the questions we should be asking. So, I include this important paper here.

Thank you, Dr. Manette, for your permission to share it with my readers.

As physicians for animals, veterinarians must contend with a paradox of power and responsibility which mirrors back to us key issues concerning the relationships between humans and animals on our planet. At the top of the list of paradoxes is our power to restrain and manipulate animals and the question of how to do so in a way that, at the very least, does no harm. This responsibility includes the paradox of life and death. As physicians, we are trained to help in nature's healing process. But we also treat our patients with the knowledge that some will ultimately be slaughtered for human use. At other times, we are called upon to perform euthanasia, and not always for humane medical reasons. To be accomplices in these acts can be deeply disturbing. But equally disturbing can be the prolongation of an animal's life when its life has been deeply compromised by trauma or a terminal illness, but whose person is not yet willing to let that life go. Indeed, it appears, as many before me have said, that science has made us gods before we have learned to be good humans.

As a veterinarian, it is impossible for me to avoid the question of whether or not part of our responsibility is to help animals deal with their own deaths, the death of one of their offspring, or a companion animal. Death comes easily for very few animals or humans. And like others, I have seen animals deeply grieve the deaths of their babies or a companion animal, and I know their pain. How can we help at such times? How can we express gratitude for the animals whose lives have been taken in the process of our learning to be their physicians? Is it even possible or desirable to express our appreciation for their feelings or our grief at their loss? How do we better understand our relationships to the animals whose lives we have taken or will take?

Each one of us who comes in contact with animals is, to one degree or another, affected by personal and cultural myths through which we filter our experiences and make sense of our worlds. As with any other issue we encounter in life, these myths have a great deal to do with our understanding of human-animal relationships. Any changes we make in those relationships may require us to look at those myths and perhaps transform them. Joseph Campbell notes in *The Power of Myth* that "ancient myths were designed to harmonize the mind and the body . . . to put the mind in accord with the body and the way of life in accord with the way that nature dictates." That we have these myths is normal and natural to facilitate our passage through life.

The myths at the center of our human-animal relationships circle around the tendency for humans to empathize with other people and animals. This is a vital and distinctive component of being human, one that enables us to reach out to others, to help ease others through their pain and sorrow, and to share their joys. Because of our highly-developed social awareness, we can personally identify with animals and want to care for them. Our capacity for empathy serves us well in the roles we have assumed as the animals' physicians. But how do we handle our desire to help and bring comfort when we are confronted with the moral and emotional dilemma of killing them or seeing them maltreated?

As part of our active mythology, we have developed a variety of ways for dealing with the inner conflicts we experience, consciously or not, when the compassion that motivates us to be partners in healing is challenged. We have learned many mental devices for distancing ourselves from such situations, sparing ourselves from the inner conflict, guilt and remorse that may result from taking an animal's life. These distancing devices include misrepresentation, detachment (also known as "compartmentalization" or a "mechanical approach"), concealment, shifting the blame, and even sadism. Anyone who starts off with a feeling for animals will soon learn that these distancing devices not only lack authenticity, but in practicing these devices, we lose our humanity.

Early on in our history, we learned to project our disowned gifts as well as our fears and self-criticisms onto others. In the former case, we may perceive other people as demigods, placing them on pedestals high above ourselves; at the opposite pole, we may deny their humanness, turning them into objects to be judged, ridiculed, condemned, or abused. People who abuse others in these ways, typically depersonalize or objectivize their victims, detaching themselves from the words and acts by which they violate other beings.

We inherently tend to anthropomorphize, to consciously or unconsciously project positive or negative human attributes onto animals. When we evaluate and judge an animal's behavior, we blind ourselves to the animal's true nature and ascribe moral values to it. For example, pedigreed dogs are supposedly morally superior to mongrels, and many people tend to give them special treatment. Similarly, we may see predators and scavengers as savage or evil. Statements such as, "That wolf deliberately and maliciously attacked my sheep," implies the wolf had evil intent and a conscious ability to choose other ways to feed itself. Because the wolf failed to choose an alternative, such reasoning goes, it deserves swift retribution. By treating animals as objects, humans are given free rein to be coercive, which in turn trains animals to fear us and focus on escape. The animal can be reduced to an intractable unit of production.

Bernard Rollin, Colorado State University professor of veterinary ethics, suggests anthropomorphism may be a psychologically necessary first stage in a veterinarian's development of moral consciousness. The second stage is to transcend anthropomorphic depictions of animals. In this second stage of developing our relationships with animals, we at last begin to recognize that they have the right to live their lives in accordance with the needs that have been programmed into them in the course of their evolutionary development.

Our impulse to anthropomorphize animals is certainly a natural one. Who has not empathized with Bambi's plight? And how many books, (e.g., *Aesop's Fables, Peter Rabbit, Winnie the Pooh, Animal Farm*) feature animals as main characters? When we perceive animals as if they are people, we are interacting with them not as objects but as entities worthy of our respect. As we mature, we learn rabbits do not write letters and bears do not fly kites. But in the process of learning from these characters, we have opened ourselves to learning about the true nature of other life forms as well as ourselves.

Projection is only one of the ways veterinarians distance themselves from their own feelings. There is also detachment, compartmentalization, or the adoption of a mechanical approach. These are all ways of isolating our feelings, of putting physical and emotional distance between our actions and our intuitive sensibilities in order to protect ourselves from experiencing the full impact of performing tasks which would otherwise cause us internal conflict. Veterinary students and euthanasia employees at humane shelters typically use detachment when interacting with animals in ways that would otherwise cause them to feel conflicted within themselves.

Compartmentalization, the term I prefer to use, is somewhat more complex. It rests solidly upon the foundation of Cartesian duality and the creation of the doctrine of human supremacy over animals. Descartes believed animals to be soulless creatures, insensate machines or *automata*, which could be nailed to boards and dissected in public with no consequence to either the animals or the humans who indulged in such practices. Accordingly, only humans were viewed as sentient beings. This created a guilt-free forum for mutilating and killing animals. Cartesian license fosters the separation of rationality from emotions and feelings, and firmly splits the connection between mind and body. Remember, it is within our bodies that we experience feelings and sensations; it is within our heads that we label the sensations. By distancing ourselves from our bodies, and thereby from our feelings, we remove ourselves from experiencing not only fear and guilt, but also empathy and compassion. Indeed, we turn ourselves into the *automata*.

Gifted animal scientist Temple Grandin, who has designed one-third of the slaughter plants in the United States, believes the place where an animal is killed is a sacred one. Her designs for these environments create an atmosphere that is as calming and compassionate as possible to ease the last living moments of these animals and their passage through death. She also advocates the use of ritual to shape and set up certain controls on people's behavior within that environment, and to help prevent people from becoming numbed, callous, or cruel, thereby falling into a mechanical approach. Everything she does is aimed at promoting respect for the animals.

In her ideal circumstances in the slaughterhouse, the killing act would be controlled by a ritual act of submission, similar to a submissive wolf exposing its throat to a dominant wolf. This submissive act would acknowledge the unknown that haunts people, especially the unknown of what happens after death. Grandin concludes that the ritual could be something very simple, such as bowing one's head or one pure moment of silence. Employing sacred ritual at such times is not a distancing device. On the contrary, it opens us to our inherent capacity for empathy and harmonious interaction, or union, with all life. The use of sacred ritual can help us to seek life, to honor the mystery of life without asking why, or seeking to dominate or control it. Rather than blunting our empathic capacity, sacred ritual can have the beneficial effect of encouraging, maintaining and promoting an attitude of respect for all of life. Sacred ritual can enhance the awareness of our actions and foster a heightened awareness of life's secrets.

Temple Grandin bows her head before she enters a slaughter plant and sometimes writes "Stairway to Heaven" or "Valhalla" on drawings of new slaughterhouse systems she is designing. Similarly, consider the Rabinical laws and prayers used in Jewish ritual slaughter, or the rituals, prayers, and animal fetishes used by Native American hunters to prepare themselves for the hunt, the actual killing, and dressing out of the dead animal.

In 1993, Alison Taylor and Hank Davis organized a memorial celebration to acknowledge the use of animals and their contribution to excellence in research and teaching at the University of Guelph in Ontario, Canada. The intention of the service was to promote discussion and a deeper awareness of the issues raised by animal care, and to take some time to reflect upon the broad implications of our dependency on the use of animals in research and education.

In May, 1999, several students attending Columbine High School in Littleton, Colorado were murdered by two of their classmates. Survivors used prayer and ritual with crosses and flowers to commemorate their classmates' deaths.

Animals have the right to life, but that right to life is not absolute, nor is it for humans. Still, the taking of a life should be acknowledged with compassion and responsibility, whatever the life form happens to be.

Fostering Empathy and Attributes of Veterinarians

How veterinarians handle these issues tells us a lot about the larger social system in which we all operate. As our human populations swell, pressing further and further into what was once the wilderness, the home of the animals, it is increasingly important for us to look at these issues. At no time in our history has it been more important for us to consciously seek a wider awareness of our relationships with other species and to seek ways of honoring all of life.

Should veterinarians foster and facilitate an empathic, sacred ritual approach to the killing of animals? There is a variety of answers to this question. Veterinarian Franklin D. MacMilan, in the *Journal of the American Veterinary Medical Association*, concluded that scientific data supports appropriate, compassionate human contact as "an adjunct treatment in health care . . . before, during, and after illness, injury, and surgery for animals that appear to respond favorably to human contact, that is, those who display no signs of fear toward human beings." He continues: "No medical act carries more importance—emotional and moral, if not scientific—than euthanasia of companion animals. This unique time requires application of every known tool to optimize animal well-being and comfort, including full use of the effects of human contact."

The importance of animals in all aspects of human life is receiving increasing attention in recent years, a much needed change in our society. Law schools at Harvard and Yale are teaching classes on animal rights. To keep abreast of contemporary changes, a complacent, value-neutral attitude is no longer either appropriate or ethical. The approach of veterinarians must mature into a more empathic one, with broader channels of professional concern, and deeper, updated ways of thinking about the interrelatedness of human beings and animals.

Physician J. A. Knight writes that, "the ethical and moral issues in veterinary medicine are broader and more complex than in human medicine. This is in part because veterinary medicine has all the human problems, along with a multitude of animal problems related to rights, suffering, legal standing, and protection that often may not even be considered as falling in the purview of ethics or values in our society. Thus the task of expanding the consciousness of society in general is a task confronting veterinary medicine."

One way for veterinarians to meet this task is for them to be more authentic in their interactions with animals, to relinquish and grow beyond their fears and the use of distancing devices. Shifting to a less anthropocentric attitude may prove challenging for some. But the changes clearly are coming. Today humanity is bombarded with messages from a variety of sources which urge us to reconsider our priorities and raise our sensitivity to our interactions with other creatures who share this planet with us. We are asked to become more conscious about the needs and welfare of other species.

Some veterinarians, more than others, are finding it easy to make this transition. But we are all being forced to examine practices to which we have never given a second thought. We may feel threatened, scared for our jobs, or simply philosophically uncomfortable. Difficult as they may be, such feelings may be a natural part of the evolution of our relationship with animals.

Ethical behavior has both cognitive and affective foundations. Requisites for being a veterinarian include intelligence and the ability for rational ethical reflection juxtaposed with equally important nonrational factors, such as dedication, integrity, independence, manual skills, vitality, love for animals, sensitivity, and a capacity for social bonding. Veterinarians must simultaneously be able to communicate as scientists, diagnosticians, and as supporters of animal welfare. How we respond to these responsibilities is a reflection of our personal and cultural biases or myths. But the well-entrenched myth of Cartesian duality asserts that love and science are irreconcilable, and that only what can be confirmed with our present means of ascertaining scientific proof is considered valid and worthy of recognition. This is a reminder to us that myths can be tools to help us grow and transcend limiting beliefs, or they can be straitjackets preventing more appropriate and ethical behavior. Myths can also calm and soothe us, like blinders focusing a horse's vision and eliminating distractions and frightening elements. But it is precisely this elimination of frightening elements that can lull us into complacency, self-deception, denial, and a false belief that our minuscule view of the world is, in reality, the view of the world.

If we are careless, we will project our myths onto others, presuming, consciously and unconsciously, that what works for us is equivalent to the truth, and therefore must be so for others. We can inappropriately define an elephant as just his tail, his trunk, his tusks or his ears, forgetting that each of these is only one tiny part of the elephant. But Elephant is the totality of these parts, and so much more.

We humans have the ability to see other viewpoints, if we so choose to expand ourselves and do so. Fostering diversity in our thinking, enhancing and broadening our understanding, and transcending our limitations has never been more critical. As we approach ways to develop a deeper understanding of all creatures on our planet, we will be asked to actively listen, to risk being more honest with ourselves, and to be open to the world of possibilities. Just as an animal can be trained to go past objects which had previously frightened it, so it is for us humans. We veterinarians can move and grow through our fears and inner conflicts, rather than being limited by devices we have developed to evade them. First, we need to recognize that we all have feelings, and some of them are uncomfortable and unpleasant. Based on our mythologies, we can react to these feelings by denying them, exiting from the experience of their full impact. Or, we can choose to act creatively—to allow ourselves to experience and stay united with our physical sensations, witnessing them in the present moment rather than pushing them away.

To accomplish the task before us, of opening up to the deeper meaning of our relationships with animals, we are at last opening up to the paradox of empathy and life-taking. Temple Grandin relates the story of operating the restraint chute during the Jewish ritual slaughter of animals. During this experience she stayed connected with her bodily sensations. She reported that, "When the animal remained completely calm I felt an overwhelming feeling of peacefulness, as if God had touched me. I did not feel bad about what I was doing. A good restraint chute operator has to not just like the cattle, but love them. Operating the chute has to be done as an act of total kindness. The more gently I was able to hold the animal with the apparatus, the more peaceful I felt. As the life force left the animal, I had deep religious feelings. For the first time in my life, logic had been completely overwhelmed with feelings I did not know I had."

By staying connected with the sensations in our bodies we can perhaps learn more about life, fear death less, and be more receptive to a broadened perception of this amazing life that surrounds us. Albert Schweitzer, believing in equality of all life forms, emphasized and practiced reverence for all life. Doing so, he believed, imbues humans with a sense of responsibility for life and leads to a will to love. Life, in and of itself, was sacred to him, regardless of whether the life has linguistic ability, intelligence comparable to humans, an ability to experience pleasure or pain, or an economic or medical benefit for humans. For Schweitzer, a person is ethical only if he is compassionate. The fact that we can hinder or help other life forms makes them inherently deserving of our moral concern, reverence, respect and love.

Biologist Edmund O. Wilson proposed that humans possess a trait broader than empathy, which he calls "biophilia." This means "the innate tendency to focus on life and lifelike processes." He argues that "to explore and affiliate with life is a deep and complicated process in mental development," concluding that we are a species that "will find little ultimate meaning apart from the remainder of life." Indeed, if we ignore this inherent capacity, we dishonor who we are, and may unwittingly embitter and diminish the quality of our personal life.

Erich Fromm writes that humankind is "biologically endowed with the capacity for biophilia." In *The Art of Loving*, Fromm cautions us that if we only analyze, dissect and manipulate the life that surrounds us in our earnest desire to learn its secrets, we will glean only a superficial understanding. To truly fathom life's secrets, we need to love all life. For Fromm, love is an active process with four basic components: care, responsibility, respect, and knowledge.

Schweitzer, Wilson, and Fromm all propose that humanity must extend the envelope of rationalism to include reverence for life and compassion if we truly are to develop our human potential. They, along with other authors mentioned in this paper, also express that we have an obligation for responsible stewardship for the animals with whom we share this planet.

Veterinarians, physicians trained to help animals, can heal themselves and serve as mediators between the human and animal worlds. Veterinarians are in a unique position to create optimal ways to interact with animals, teaching and encouraging responsible animal care and handling. They can foster and facilitate the expression of biophilia, reverence for life, and promote the use of sacred rituals to enhance our sense of responsibility, respect, and compassion when we interact with animals, particularly when animals are killed. With such a caring approach, we express gratitude to the animals from whom we derive so much benefit. More than that, we honor our inherent capacity to affiliate with all life and more fully develop as humans. We express an act of submission to the mystery and secret of life, learn to fear our own deaths less, and harmonize more intimately with all life forms, humans included. Our choice to act either unconsciously or consciously, with distancing devices or love, will likely color the responses of our clients, define our relationships with them, and forecast how well the animals for whom we are care-takers will be able to heal themselves. In serving the animals in these ways, we perhaps serve all of Creation a little more fully.

References

Campell, J., *The Power of Myth*. New York: Doubleday, 1988.

Fromm, E., *The Anatomy of Human Destructiveness*. New York: Holt, Rinehart, and Winston, 1973.

————. *The Art of Loving*, 2nd ed. New York: Harper and Row, 1956.

Grandin, T., "Behavior of Slaughter Plant and Auction Employees towards the Animals." *Anthrozoos* 1988; 1:205-213.

————. *Thinking in Pictures*. New York: Vintage Books, 1995.

————. "Humanitarian Aspects of *Shehitah* in the United States." *Judaism*, 1990; 39:536.

Herzog, H.A. Vore, T.L., New, Jr. J.C., "Conversations with Veterinary Students: Attitudes, Ethics, and Animals." *Anthrozoos*, 1989; 2:181-188.

Knight, J.A., "The Sacred, the Profane, and Hippocrates in Matters of Medical Ethics." *Journal of Veterinary Medical Etihcs*, 1983; 9:107-110.

Lawrence, E.A., "Love for Animals and the Veterinary Profession." *Journal of the American Veterinary Medical Association*. 1994; 205:970-972.

————. "Is Love for Animals Our Best Motivation in the Veterinary Profession?" *Massvet News* 1991; 6-7.

McMillan, F.D., "Effects of Human Contact on Animal Health and Well-being." *Journal of the American Veterinary Medical Association*. 1999; 215:1592-1598.

Owens, C.E., Davis, R, Smith, B.H., "The Psychology of Euthanizing Animals: The Emotional Components." *International Journal for the Study of Animal Problems*, 1981; 2:19-27.

Rollin B., *Animal Rights and Human Morality*. Buffalo, NY: Prometheus Books, 1981.

Serpell, J., *In the Company of Animals*. New York: Basil Blackwell, 1986.

Taylor, A., Davis, H., "Acknowledging Animals: a Memorial Service for Teaching and Research Animals." *Anthrozoos* 1993; 6:221-225.

Annotated Bibliography

Andrews, Lynn V., *Love and Power: Awakening to Mastery*. N.Y.: HarperCollins, 1997.

Though best known for her books on shamanic wisdom, in this one she explores sources of wisdom and power reflected in our friendships. It is a profound and moving exploration of love and personal power. For anyone who wants to explore the issues of personal power, and to better understand how they manifest in our lives, this book is highly recommended.

Ausubel, Ken, *Restoring the Earth: Visionary Solutions from the Bioneers*. Tiburon, Calif.: H.J.Kramer, 1997.

In this book we are introduced to the key concepts of the "Bioneers," a worldwide movement aimed at restoring the Earth and redefining our relationship with all our fellow inhabitants.

Baldwin, Christina, *Calling the Circle: The First and Future Culture*, New York: Bantam Books, 1998.

Bataille, Georges, Austrin Wainhouse, tr. *Lascaux: Prehistoric Painting or the Birth of Art*. Lausanne, France: Skira, 1955.

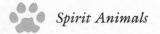

Bennett, Hal Zina, *Zuni Fetishes: Using Native American Objects for Meditation, Reflection and Insight.* N.Y.: Harper Collins,1993.

I recommend this book because it's mine but also because I know that it has helped tens of thousands of readers better understand the importance of animal spirits as teachers. Inspired by the ancient religious practices of the Zuni Indians, it tells how the spirit animals can be accessed through the help of the small, stone carvings of animals, for which the Zuni people are famous.

Bennett, Hal Zina, *The Lens of Perception.* Berkeley, Calif.: Celestial Arts, 1989.

(Watch for a new edition of this book.) It provides a clear picture of how the shaman sees beyond everyday human perception into the invisible realities that govern our lives. Contains a "how to" section for incorporating these practices into your own life.

Bennett, Hal Zina, *Spirit Circle: A Story of Adventure and Shamanic Revelation.* Ukiah, Calf.: Tenacity Press, 1998.

This is a prophetic novel, much of which came to me through dreams and visions. While there is a serious prophecy contained in this book, with a lot about the practice of shamanism, readers have said that it is an exciting story with great characters. It is perhaps the only novel in existence with a "how to" section in the back, helping readers to incorporate the prophecy into their own lives.

Bennett, Hal Zina, "Creativity and the Heart of Shamanism," published in *The Soul of Creativity: Insights Into the Creative Process.* edited by Tona Pearce Myers, Novato, Calif.: New World Library, 1999.

This is an essay in an excellent collection of writers on the spiritual aspects of creativity. I think it is important reading for anyone who wants to explore the role of creativity in spiritual development.

Buffalo Horn Man, Gary and Sherry Firedancer, *Animal Energies*. Spokane, W.A: Dancing Otter Publishing, 1992.
A short but excellent little chapbook describing characteristics of 58 animals, derived mostly from the authors' observations of the animals in nature. It's a good reference to explore what dream animals might be trying to teach you. If you can't find their book in the bookstore, contact them at: DanceOtter@aol.com.

Campbell, Joseph, *Myths to Live By*, New York: Viking Press, 1972.

Cowan, Tom, *Shamanism As A Spiritual Practice for Daily Life*. Freedom, Calif.: The Crossing Press, 1996.
This is one of the most down to earth books around for integrating shamanism in modern life. He provides excellent instructions for rituals and practices that can help you explore this ancient, Nature-based form of spirituality.

Eliade, Mircea, Willard R. Trask, tr. *Shamanism: Archaic Techniques of Ecstasy*, London: Arkana, 1989.

Eagle Feather, Ken, *A Toltec Path*. Charlottesville, V.A.: Hampton Roads Publishing Company, 1995.
Inspired by Carlos Castenada's writings, Ken has pursued the Toltec Path as a personal spiritual practice. He teaches in the U.S. and Europe and continues to be perhaps the best informed writer and teacher of this way. This book contains both wonderful information and clear instructions for the practice of Toltec principles. "Must" reading for anyone serious about pursuing a deeper knowledge of Earth-based spirituality.

Graham, David E., "Desert Reveals an Old-time Religion," *The New York Times*, May 18, 1998.

Grof, Stanislav, M.D. with Hal Zina Bennett, *The Holotropic Mind: The Three Levels of Human Consciousness and How They Shape Our Lives.* N.Y.: HarperCollins, 1992.
    Stan Grof is perhaps the most highly respected researcher of altered states of consciousness and how dreams, the unconscious, and "other realities" affect our lives. Bestselling author Fred Alan Wolf called him "the most brilliant mind in psychology today . . . " I had the great honor of working with him on this book, and I recommend it and his other books for anyone who wants to know more about what shamans call the "invisible reality."

Hillman, James and Margo McLean, *Dream Animals*. San Francisco: Chronicle Books, 1997.
    I love this book, partly because of Margo McLean's wonderful, full-color artwork throughout. She and Hillman explore the meaning and purpose of animals in our lives. Like the best books and the best art, it provides no answers, but does open windows to show the vast landscape beyond consensual reality. A treasure of a book.

Horn, Gabriel (White Deer of Autumn), *Contemplations of a Primal Mind*. Novato, Calif.: New World Library, 1996.
    Horn explores the question, "What is the 'primal mind,' and what is the 'civilized mind?'" bringing in discussions of the awesome experiences of those who see the miracles and splendors, and the spirits of the supernatural realms. He inspires readers to honor our sacred interconnectedness with all life on our planet and all that lives here—plant, animal, Mother Earth Herself, and human.

Jung, C.G., *Memories, Dreams, Reflections*, New York: Vintage Books, 1965.

Kennedy, Eugene, "Earthrise: The Dawning of a New Spiritual Awareness," *The New York Times Magazine*, April 15, 1979.

O'Leary, Brian, Ph.D., *Exploring Inner and Outer Space*, Berkley, Calif.: North Atlantic Books, 1989.

Matthews, John, *Taliesin: Shamanism and the Bardic Mysteries in Britain and Ireland*. London: Aquarian Press, 1991.

Dense writing in the European scholarly tradition, this book takes us into the world of Celtic shamanism and spiritual practices. It has been important to me if only to better understand the relationship between nature and spirituality that is at the base of those of us who are from European backgrounds, but who find truth in Earth-based religions.

McGaa, Ed (Eagle Man), *Mother Earth Spirituality: Native American Paths to Healing Ourselves and Our World*. San Francisco: Harper and Row, 1990.

The author of this book, a Oglala Sioux lawyer, writer and lecturer, here presents teachings that he feels are essential for anyone to learn if they are concerned about healing our relationship with Mother Earth. Clear, informative, and generous in its substance, this is important reading.

Rivers, Frank, *The Way of the Owl: Succeeding with Integrity in a Conflicted World*, San Francisco: HarperSanFrancisco 1996.

Using the Owl as a teacher and metaphor, the author of this little book explores lessons for life that he has learned from observing this animal in nature. Contains short lessons for life, on everything from learning the art of falling, to thinking like a forest, and confronting the ultimate enemy. Great examples of the animals' lessons.

Solisti-Mattleton, Kate, *Conversations with Dog*. Portland, Ore.: Beyond Words Publishing, 2000.

An animal communicator, Kate has had a lot of experience working very closely with animals. This book contains wonderful insights into the emotional and spiritual needs of dogs. It's actually a very practical book, with insights about our "best friend" which are down to Earth while taking us into the minds of dogs.

————, Patrice Mattleton, *The Holistic Animal Handbook*. Portland, Ore.: Beyond Words Publishing, 2000.

This holistic guide brings together a great deal of information for the care of the animals who share our homes with us. There's abundant information about nutrition, training, emotional balancing, and communicating with animals. Includes sections on both dogs and cats, covering vitamins and minerals, organic foods, and even Bach flower remedies. There's also a section on animal communication.

Smith, Huston, *The World's Religions: Our Great Wisdom Traditions*. San Francisco, HarperSanFrancisco, 1991.

Sun Bear, C. Mulligan, P. Nufer, and Wabun, *Walk in Balance: The Path to Healthy, Happy, Harmonious Living*. New York: Prentice Hall, 1989.

Tobias, Michael and Kate Solisti-Mattelon, *Kinship With the Animals*. Hillsboro, Oregon: Beyond Words Publishing, 1998.

An anthology of essays about our relationships with animals, including pieces by Jane Goodall, Gabriel Horn, Michael Roads, and Linda Tellington-Jones.

Index

About the Author

This is Hal Zina Bennett's fifth book on nature-based spirituality and shamanism. Born and raised in Michigan, his shamanic path started in 1952 after a coma and near death experience that changed his life and left him temporarily blind. In his search to understand what he had experienced during his encounter with death, he pursued paths on both the dark and light sides of life. He eventually found clarity in the 1960s and 1970s during apprenticeships with shamans who taught with entheogens. In the 1980s, Hal committed himself to a disciplined study of shamanism. The nature-based principles he describes in this book have been the heart of his spiritual practice for nearly twenty years.

Hal and his wife, Susan J. Sparrow, live in a tiny village near a small lake in Northern California. They teach workshops on nature-based spirituality, write, coach other writers, and run their own publishing company, Tenacity Press.

For Further Information

Halbooks@HalZinaBennett.com
Or phone: 1-707-275-9011
On the web at: www.HalZinaBennett.com

Hampton Roads Publishing Company

. . . for the evolving human spirit

HAMPTON ROADS PUBLISHING COMPANY publishes books
on a variety of subjects, including spirituality,
health, and other related topics.

For a copy of our latest trade catalog,
call 978-465-0504,
or visit our website www.hrpb.com